TESOL VOICES

INSIDER ACCOUNTS OF CLASSROOM LIFE

ONLINE AND HYBRID CLASSROOM EDUCATION

EDITOR, **GREG KESSLER**

SERIES EDITOR, **TIM STEWART**

www.tesol.org/bookstore

TESOL International Association
1925 Ballenger Avenue
Alexandria, Virginia, 22314 USA
www.tesol.org

Director of Publishing and Product Development: Myrna Jacobs
Copy Editor: Tomiko Breland
Cover and Interior Design: Citrine Sky Design
Layout: Capitol Communications, LLC
Printing: Gasch Printing, LLC

ISBN 9781942799788
Library of Congress Control Number 2017943455

Table of Contents

Series Editor's Preface

The TESOL Voices series aims to fill the need for expanding practical knowledge through participant research in the field. Each volume showcases the voices of students and teachers engaged in participant inquiry about language education. These inquiries of participants in various TESOL learning environments are told as insider accounts of discovery, challenge, change, and growth.

What constitutes TESOL classroom life and who is best positioned to research this unique ecology? Traditionally, there has been a hierarchy of credibility in TESOL encouraging the production of knowledge by credentialed "experts" in higher education who offer TESOL practitioners outsider understandings about teaching. In contrast, the TESOL Voices series presents insider accounts from students and teachers who are theorizing the practices of both learning and teaching for themselves. In other words, this series positions practice ahead of theory for understanding the complex phenomena of language teaching and learning. In short, the TESOL Voices series seeks to elevate the value of localized learning through classroom research.

In this series, readers will discover relevant strands of theory extending from accounts of practice. The philosophical point of departure for the series is that enduring theory in TESOL is most likely to surface from participant inquiry that happens among the clutter of classroom desks and chairs. As participants tell their stories, reflective questions and implications for language teaching emerge that illustrate the practical theory practitioners use to make decisions as they experience classroom life.

The TESOL Voices series attempts to give readers a view from the classroom floor on the appropriateness of current policy, practice, and theory in language education. While the accounts in these books are personal reflections colored by particular contexts, teachers are likely to find parallels with their own situation. So as you read, listen carefully to discover what the murmurs, echoes, articulations, singing, humming, silence, cries, laughter, and voices that flow from each of the six volumes might teach you.

Insider Accounts From Online and Hybrid Classrooms

This volume demonstrates the rich diversity currently available for English study and teaching in online and hybrid environments. Chapters in this volume are organized in the following sections: teacher preparation, ESL and EFL online teaching and learning, and ESL and EFL hybrid teaching and learning. Reflective teaching and participant inquiry are featured throughout the book. Specific chapter topics include formalized course training to help teachers deal with the new technologies that are entering schools, mentorship practices, developing learner autonomy, flipped-classroom formats, and the potential of social networking for language learning. Chapter authors in this volume truly are trailblazers in the dynamic frontier of teaching and learning technology. This book of insider accounts is a must for TESOL practitioners who want to stay abreast of developments for online and hybrid classrooms. The concluding chapter is a broad reflection on where the field currently stands and where it appears to be heading. This volume is a solid attempt at anticipating both student and teacher needs as all participants in language classrooms adjust to technological change.

Tim Stewart, Kyoto University

Introduction: A Diversity of Online and Hybrid TESOL Voices

GREG KESSLER

H ybrid and online learning have been around for some time and many of us across educational domains have had experience teaching and learning in these contexts. However, not all online environments and practices are created equal. The breadth of these contexts today requires us to carefully reflect upon our practices to better understand the various ways that we can interact with one another in the pursuit of effective teaching and learning. There is evidence that many factors may influence how technologies are implemented, including cultural norms and expectations. Similarly, the educational backgrounds of teachers and learners and their attitudes toward these approaches, and technology in general, can determine if a given technological intervention will have any chance of success. As we learn more about these online and hybrid contexts, we continue to develop a richer and more sophisticated understanding. The chapters in this volume have much to contribute to this discussion. This volume in the TESOL Voices series addresses reflective teaching practices and participant inquiry in online and hybrid teaching contexts. The authors in this collection present a diversity of authentic TESOL teaching and learning contexts utilizing online and hybrid instructional approaches. Each chapter is illustrated with a rich description of participant inquiry.

This is a collection of insider perspectives that is geographically, culturally, and contextually diverse. The collection is divided into three sections: (1) voices of participants in online and hybrid TESOL teacher preparation contexts, (2) voices of participants in online ESL and EFL contexts, and (3) voices of participants in hybrid ESL and EFL contexts.

Voices From Online and Hybrid TESOL Teacher Preparation Contexts

The first section begins with a chapter that vividly illustrates the importance of participant inquiry. In the chapter, **Andrei and Salerno** share their personal stories through the lens of collaborative activity as instructors with shared experiences of, interests in, and explorations of teaching online.

They describe their partnership, one formed by colleagues who might otherwise be isolated, based on a personal linguistic bond that has been maintained for years online. These inspiring authors employ the same principles that helped them maintain this relationship to their online teaching. They offer suggestions for harnessing the power of collaboration to enhance the experience of both MA TESOL candidates and teacher trainers.

Chapter 2 takes us to an online TESOL teacher preparation course that allows MA candidates to participate from anywhere in the world. **Gilmetdinova, de Oliveira, and Olesova** present the voices of an instructor, a teaching assistant, and a student to describe their design, implementation, and evaluation of specific interactive tools within Blackboard, a virtual learning environment and course management system, to strive toward an improved learning experience for students in a fully online context. They observe that the use of tools that support voice-based interactions can help to support teaching presence and contribute to the maintenance of a human connection. The chapter illustrates the importance of reciprocity throughout the educational process and offers guidance for others who are considering wholly online TESOL courses and programs.

In Chapter 3, **Ates and Graham** present the reflective voices of graduate students and faculty about their experiences in an online MA TESOL program. The authors describe this experience and share a number of practical recommendations for both students and faculty. These recommendations are not only thorough and practical but should also be useful for students and teachers in many other online contexts.

In Chapter 4, **Guler** explores the challenges mainstream teachers of ELLs face. She provides insight into the distinct needs of this often overlooked constituency and offers recommendations for addressing their concerns. Through the voices of these teachers, we can appreciate how these challenges are addressed. Guler also shares implications for how online teacher education can help better prepare teachers to effectively address the needs of ELLs.

Voices From Online ESL and EFL Contexts

The second section includes chapters focused on the voices of participants in online ESL and EFL contexts. This section begins in Chapter 5 with **Casal and Lee** exploring the discourse practices of tutoring within a fully online context through the reflective dialogue of a tutor and his mentor. They recognize that such practices are becoming increasingly important as online and hybrid teaching becomes increasingly commonplace and technologies provide greater support for "sustainable synchronous one-on-one interactions." They observe that "reflection can lead to a profound awareness of personal discourse practices," particularly as they manifest in online writing lab spaces, and guide tutors toward more effective practice. Such awareness can benefit all of us who engage in these emerging online contexts.

In Chapter 6, **Chang and Windeatt** present a framework for creating and delivering online English for academic purposes courses. This framework is informed by a number of established frameworks and the observations of teacher and learner use of the Moodle learning management software at the authors' institution. They share the voices of students and faculty within a course, with a focus on evaluating course design through the use of this framework, and they outline the benefits of this approach and provide suggestions for expansion of the framework. Their process and recommendations should help readers reflect more thoughtfully on future online course design projects.

In Chapter 7, **Lima** describes an investigation into learners' perspectives of an innovative approach to teaching pronunciation through the use of an online tutoring system. She shares the voices of students using a tool that she developed, Supra Tutor, intended to improve the comprehensibility of international teaching assistants in an online, self-paced environment. Lima includes student experience with and reflection on the use of this online environment and concludes with suggestions for future improvements that may support learner autonomy. This chapter should also prove useful for others who are creating their own innovative solutions to challenging situations.

Voices From Hybrid ESL and EFL Contexts

The third section of this volume includes chapters focused on the voices of participants in hybrid ESL and EFL contexts. In Chapter 8, **Lee and Nakamura** describe the experience of participants in a videoconference-based flipped class in Japan. With a focus on advocating for an English as an international language (EIL) perspective, the authors focus on the use of videoconferencing as a pedagogical method. They describe this implementation in response to various challenges presented by this particular teaching context. The chapter concludes with suggestions for others, including combining EIL with content language integrated learning and applying EIL concepts to computer-assisted language learning teacher education.

For a student-centered perspective, Chapter 9 takes us to a Japanese EFL course constructed around self- and peer-reviewing activities facilitated through the exchange of mobile video. **Toland and Mills** present the common scenario of a Japanese-based English-teaching context in which students are extremely reluctant to speak publicly but are expected to master the skill. The authors illustrate how they constructed alternative approaches that are much less intimidating for these students in a course they describe as a metareflection instructional model intended to improve students' public speaking and presentation skills, and they share students' perceptions. Having taught in this context myself, I recognize the challenges they face quite clearly and applaud their creative intervention.

In Chapter 10, **Downer and Daleure** present a flipped-classroom environment in which students at a technical university in the United Arab Emirates participate in experiential learning, including hands-on activities such as the creation of a Rube-Goldberg machine, based on the relevance of and student interest around topics. These activities are constructed upon reading and writing skills designed to "engage them in interesting and relevant activities." The voices of students and instructors describe this culturally contextualized approach. This is followed by advice from former graduate students regarding an online MA TESOL program.

In Chapter 11, **Rashid** presents an innovative online peer mentoring project using Facebook to promote autonomy among Malaysian preservice teachers. This use of social media allows students to engage in an informal mentoring relationship while allowing those who are more knowledgeable or experienced to provide guidance for those who are less so. Rashid describes the participants' reflections on the peer mentoring process and the potential for using social network sites such as Facebook for such pursuits.

In Chapter 12, I reflect on these studies and present an overview of various developments that are underway in instructional technology, CALL, and language education. These are described with a focus on how these developments may influence hybrid and online teaching and learning.

Throughout these chapters, readers will note the conviction and passion of the authors and participants. As we embrace these new teaching and learning contexts, it is comforting to know there is so much commitment and creativity among those leading the way. I am confident that readers will be inspired by the voices and reflections captured throughout this volume.

....

Greg Kessler is an associate professor of instructional technology and linguistics at Ohio University.

SECTION 1:
VOICES FROM ONLINE AND HYBRID TESOL TEACHER PREPARATION CONTEXTS

1

Collaborative Practice to Improve How ELLs Are Characterized in Online TESOL Methods Courses

ELENA ANDREI AND APRIL S. SALERNO

Online Disconnect

Though online environments certainly have potential to—and do—connect people across great distances, we have found that online teaching can ironically feel like an isolated endeavor. People have long said that teaching can be lonely in regular classroom settings: Once a teacher shuts the door, he or she is "alone." Fortunately, educators—specifically language teachers—have made strides in finding innovative ways to establish collaborative relationships within physical schools and universities, through inquiry (Cochran-Smith & Lytle, 2009), communities of practice (Wenger, 2009), and various approaches to collaborative teaching (Gladman, 2015; Martin-Beltrán & Peercy, 2012). In online teaching, however, being alone takes on an additional dimension, with feelings of isolation a primary challenge of online instruction (Wilson et al., 2003). No longer is the teacher alone in front of a class of students in a physical institution; there are no hallways where you might run into another faculty member and talk about practice. Instead, being alone might actually mean sitting by yourself at your computer, possibly miles apart from students, with little or no connection to other teachers.

This, at least, seemed to be our situation. As learners of each other's first language, we had not only formed a close friendship in graduate school but also had begun questioning together how educators depict language learners. After graduation, we found ourselves as young instructors teaching separate online courses miles apart at different institutions, at first in different U.S. states and later in different countries. Through occasional video-conferencing conversations, we came to realize we were doing similar work, facing similar challenges. We were both teaching online courses on TESOL to practicing and preservice teachers pursuing TESOL certifications. We both valued talking positively about English language learners (ELLs). And we both faced tricky situations in trying to facilitate and shape our students' online, asynchronous discussions to that end. After recognizing our mutual, separate struggles, a collaborative relationship naturally emerged. Next, we share our stories of learning.

Positioning Ourselves Within the Narrative

Elena's Story

I am a nonnative English speaker, or an ELL, or a bilingual. Sometimes I do not know which label to use to describe myself and my linguistic and cultural abilities. I grew up learning and speaking Romanian, and I did part of my academic work in Romanian. I learned English as a foreign language (EFL) in my native country; now I am using English as a second language (ESL) daily while teaching in the United States. I have been an EFL and ESL teacher, as well as an international student and a faculty member, so I can say I have various life and professional experiences with using and developing ESL skills.

I met April when we were doctoral students. She was the first non-Romanian I met who speaks Romanian. It brought tears to my eyes hearing her speak Romanian because I regarded it as a great compliment and honor for me, my language, and my country. During graduate school, April was my language and cultural guide, helping me with the language and cultural intricacies that were new and unfamiliar.

I love teaching online, which is not the case for everyone, but even I sometimes felt alone with my class (that is, sitting at my computer) trying to determine how to talk (that is, write) to my students and unsure how to respond to posts that might portray emergent bilinguals in deficit-oriented ways (García & Kleifgen, 2018). I believe both April and I have the basic mechanics of teaching online figured out: We create online learning communities in which students interact asynchronously; we participate actively in forums; we write wrap-up announcements at the end of each forum; we maintain consistency across weeks by having a weekly overview, objectives, and tasks; and we encourage students to share their expertise and experiences. But I've found that when I have to address misconceptions about ELLs, I need a peer "buddy." In those moments, I wonder: How do I tactfully address these misconceptions in the forums, when everyone, not just the teacher with the misconception, can read the post? How do I address misconceptions while still valuing teachers and helping them save face (Goffman, 1955)?

April's Story

Elena and I are linked not only through our scholastic interests but also our common languages, both figuratively and literally. We both speak English and Romanian. For me, English is my first language. I learned Romanian as a Peace Corps volunteer 15 years ago in the Republic of Moldova, a former Soviet state bordering Elena's native Romania. When Elena and I met as doctoral students, I had just visited the campus international office to ask if they knew of any Romanian speakers with whom I might practice language; they didn't. So I was surprised at our initial orientation to find ourselves within a cohort of only six doctoral students.

Since graduating, we have moved miles, even countries apart. Like Elena, I have also lived and worked in my second language environment. Though my online courses are through my U.S. institution, I worked as an international scholar in Moldova. The beauty of online work is that it travels easily across distances. Through collaboration with Elena, we have often discussed what it means to be called an English learner. This question affects not only our identities but also how we talk in online environments with teacher-education students who are, in turn, discussing pre-K–12 ELLs in their classrooms. We certainly talked about this question of naming back in graduate school. It is a nuanced discussion even in face-to-face settings with added sensitivities necessary, as we have found, in online environments. We are far from the first to have this conversation. In conceptualizing our inquiry work, we draw heavily from literature affirming that emergent bilinguals (García & Kleifgen, 2018) should be regarded for the many linguistic and cultural resources they bring to classrooms—rather than being perpetually cast as learners (Valdés, Kibler, & Walqui, 2014).

It was through my talks with Elena that I realized I had also personally taken on the identity of a language learner. I realized that whenever anyone in Moldova asked me if I spoke Romanian, I always answered, "*Încerc* (I try)." Elena helped me question that response: Why did I not simply respond, "*Da* (Yes)"?

> ❝ If I myself, as an adult with years of immersion, school success, and specialization in language study, have difficulty presenting myself as proficient in my second language, how can children or adolescents studying English portray and envision themselves as proficient, especially when living and studying in the U.S. system that constantly portrays them as learners? ❞

How can we help teachers we teach—sometimes themselves monolingual English speakers—understand these concerns, through the indirect medium of online study? It is this type of questioning that Elena and I are applying to our online courses.

Collaborating Online

As collaborative partners, we are working simultaneously toward two goals: (1) We are researching our practice with the intent of building knowledge about how instructors can shape online environments toward positive-oriented—rather than deficit-oriented (García & Kleifgen, 2018)—discourse, and (2) we are working as "critical friends" (Heath & Street, 2008) toward improving our own teaching practices in facilitating online discussions.

Through this process, not only are we available to talk with each other when we are flummoxed about how to respond to online discussion posts; we are also systematically reviewing each other's course sites and watching for instances of deficit-oriented language. We are using an approach informed by discourse analysis (Bloome et al., 2008; Gee, 2014) to help us consider how meaning was constructed in online conversations and how we might better shape that conversation in the future. Our emphasis in this inquiry is not to affirm that we are good teachers but instead to look for ways of becoming better teachers, specifically online instructors, and in this sense to keep for ourselves a growth-oriented mindset (Dweck, 2007).

Sample Online Discussion

To illustrate the kind of work we are doing, we present a sample excerpt from the first week of April's TESOL course on assessment and curriculum design. Because this was the beginning of the course and because it was expected that some students were taking an online course for the first time, learning objectives for the discussion include not only TESOL content but also understanding posting mechanics.

In the forum, April asked students to react to Gibbons's (2009) seven intellectual practices. Prior to this passage, Miriam[1] had posted an initial discussion of Gibbons's practices—describing how she uses interactive notebooks to help fourth-graders think like experts, one of Gibbons's practices. In responding to Miriam, students began a secondary conversation about pull-out and push-in instruction. We coded this discussion as one for our own analysis because of the highlighted sentence in Response 5 (emphasis added):

---

[1] All student names are pseudonyms.

Re: Diving into Gibbons' seven practices

[1] Jessica (Tuesday 4:17 am)

Hi Miriam. Do you mainly provide push in or pull out services? I mainly teach pull out, but I push in for a 3rd grade social studies class. The interactive notebook sounds like it could work really well in this scenario. What types of activities do your students do in these notebooks?

[2] Miriam (Tuesday 7:40 pm)

Hi Jessica,

There is no pull out services at the school that I work at. There is only push in. The interactive notebooks have a teacher side and then a student side that directly correlates to the other one. We put the teacher side on the right and then student side is on the left. It varies on how they appear and the content. [. . .]

[3] Elizabeth (Wednesday 8:37 am)

Hi Miriam,

I am new to the world of ELL and am not familiar with some terms. I understand pull out services, but is [sic] push in? Does it mean, giving the student one-on-one help by an ESL teacher in the classroom?

[4] Jessica (Wednesday 10:16 pm)

Hi Miriam,

"Push in" is when a teacher—ESOL, Special Ed, or Reading, provide [sic] services to the students in their regular classroom. I'm not sure if this is a formal term, but it is the phrase that is used in the county I teach in.

[5] Miriam (Thursday 6:20 pm)

Push in, is when a supporting teacher comes into the classroom to work with students. I currently have an ELL teacher that works with me throughout the day and an ELL aid. There is support in the classroom throughout the day. The ELL aid is not allowed to do guided reading with a group because she has not been formally trained in it. However, she does work in a small group setting. **Since the majority of the students are ELLs she works with the lowest students.** She does work with the other students. I think that I may have made more of a confusion.

Analysis

The two of us analyzed and discussed the passage together through an asynchronous electronic discussion. Because the excerpt was from April's course, she began our discussion by posing questions to Elena:

(1) Do you think that Elizabeth left the conversation with an understanding of the difference between push-in and pull-out? If not, what misunderstandings might she have? As a teacher, what could I have done to clear those up? (2) What do you think that Miriam is saying in the highlighted passage in Response 5? (3) What ideas do you have for how I could insert myself in this conversation?

In her response, Elena answered these questions before posing additional questions to April. Our discussion continued in this way until both of us felt our questions had been resolved and that we had no new questions. Eventually, we came up with the following three conclusions.

1. *It was unclear whether Elizabeth had an improved understanding of "push-in" and "pull-out" instruction and that April as the instructor could have clarified this issue.*

We considered that Elizabeth's question was a call for factual information and that it would be appropriate for April to enter the discussion and provide resources for answering the question. This information was not part of the week's learning objectives, and Elizabeth did not post the question to the course site's forum, which April specifically set up for asking questions. But the literature supports the value of "teachable moments" as opportunities for teaching and learning (Hyun & Marshall, 2003) when teachers might exercise sensitivity and provide quality feedback (Pianta, Hamre, & Mintz, 2011). April was reluctant to jump into the discussion because she did not want to squash students' opportunities to position themselves as experts and because she tries in her teaching to disrupt the traditional initiation-response-evaluation order of classroom discussions (Bloome et al., 2008): "You know, this makes me think about the [initiation-response-evaluation] cycle, and how I try to disrupt that and avoid being the teacher with the answer in the end of a face-to-face discussion." Elena pointed out that carefully crafted language can help further discussion, without overpowering students' posts: "I like to be very diplomatic and I would say something like, 'To add to what Jessica and Miriam are saying. . .'" The question of how teachers and students are positioned as holders of knowledge in online discussions is one we continue to explore in our ongoing research.

2. *The online context is reflected in the excerpt.*

As we paid careful attention to this excerpt, we noticed that in Response 4, Jessica apparently mistakenly responds to Miriam instead of Elizabeth. Although Miriam posted initially, Elizabeth asked the question about pull-out versus push-in. April did not notice this misnaming while teaching that week. In our analysis of the discussion, we considered the possibility that this might be because students are in their first week and are still learning each other's names. We believe that it might also be related to the format of online discussions, in which respondents can lose track of who posted in which thread.

Elena commented: "In online instruction it is more difficult to keep track of names and if they are also learning the online format of the class, then it might be that they got lost in reading." Because we both believe in building positive classroom climates (Pianta et al., 2011), whether in face-to-face or virtual environments, noticing this mistake, minor as it seems, speaks to us about the importance of helping students build community. One way we do that is by introducing ourselves and asking students to do the same, offering professional and personal information about ourselves, as we might do in an "ice-breaker" at the start of a face-to-face class. After our discussions about this excerpt, April also decided to adopt Elena's practice of encouraging students to post pictures of themselves to help indicate who is "speaking."

3. *There are larger discussion issues that April could bring up related to Miriam's description of ELLs as "the lowest students."*

Finally, our discussion led us to consider several possibilities of what Miriam might have meant in referring to ELLs as "the lowest students." April said: "I didn't respond directly to this, but looking back, I think that I really overlooked that in the hurry to get opening-week logistics taken care of." This comment also reflects our previous point that the online context of the class affected the discussion.

Additionally, Elena saw how Miriam's post reveals that a classroom aid, rather than Miriam as a fully licensed teacher, is largely teaching the ELLs. This statement echoes research that ELLs often receive fewer resources in schools (Darling-Hammond, 2010). Further, Elena pointed out that Miriam's language is akin to national standardization discourse characterizing students by perceived measurable achievements. The question thus remained whether April should have addressed the statement in the moment. Elena noted:

> ❝ So, I think like in pre-K–12 schools and with feedback we need not to correct everything and pick our battles. . . . This is what I think: These are wonderful teachers who are interested in ELLs and want to perfect their teaching so ELLs can really learn. We do not want to scare them off, we want to manage the situation/discussion in a delicate way and make them jump to the conclusions themselves. ❞

Through our continued discussions, we thought of ways we could better manage learning without entering the discussion every time as correctors. April suggested setting discussion norms in this first week. We both regularly practice setting discussion norms with our face-to-face courses, but we had never done so with our online courses. Additionally, we decided we would bring up two issues from this excerpt later for whole-class discussion: first, the issue that teaching assistants, rather than fully certified teachers, might more often teach ELLs; and second, possible effects on ELLs of being labeled as "low" or "deficient." We could easily think of literature to provide on these topics. We could even ask students to go back and examine their own language in discussion posts.

Conclusion

Through our collaboration, we have created new space to examine and improve our teaching in ways that are difficult to achieve during the regular pace of online courses. Our partnership stemmed from the need for collaboration when feeling isolated as online TESOL instructors. Our collaboration grew out of our common situations and interests, as language learners ourselves and as TESOL teacher educators uncertain of how to steer online discussion away from labels and toward positive depictions of ELLs. We acknowledge that in training future TESOL professionals, we have the responsibility to ensure teachers' views toward ELLs do not harm students' identities, including how these students see themselves and how they want to be seen (Gee, 2014). In online environments, teaching teachers about the language they use to describe students must be interwoven across the course, not in isolated modules. Our collaborative process helps us improve our practice for the future. For example, after April noted that she missed an opportunity to correct Elizabeth, Elena responded:

> You see, as you mentioned in your other comment, in online and the first week, you can be busy, busy, and we can lose or overlook nuances. That is why this project of ours is so important. Now that we look in detail and at what the students said and why they might have said that and what we could have done, it sensitizes us for later when we see something similar.

Elena Andrei is a former ESL and EFL teacher and is currently an assistant professor of TESOL and TESOL program coordinator at Cleveland State University, Cleveland, Ohio, USA.

April S. Salerno was formerly a Fulbright Scholar at Ion Creangă State Pedagogical University in Moldova and is currently an assistant professor of TESOL at the University of Virginia, Charlottesville, Virginia, USA.

References

Bloome, D., Carter, S. P., Christian, B. M., Madrid, S., Otto, S., Shuart-Faris, N., & Smith, M. (2008). *On discourse analysis in classrooms: Approaches to language and literacy research.* New York, NY: Teachers College Press.

Cochran-Smith, M., & Lytle, S. L. (2009). *Inquiry as stance.* New York, NY: Teachers College Press.

Darling-Hammond, L. (2010). *The flat world and education: How America's commitment to equity will determine our future.* New York, NY: Teachers College Press.

Dweck, C. S. (2007). *Mindset: The new psychology of success.* New York, NY: Ballantine Books.

García, O., & Kleifgen, J. A. (2018). *Educating emergent bilinguals: Policies, programs, and practices for English learners* (2nd ed.). New York, NY: Teachers College Press.

Gee, J. P. (2014). *An introduction to discourse analysis: Theory and method.* New York, NY: Routledge.

Gibbons, P. (2009). *English learners, academic literacy, and thinking: Learning in the challenge zone.* Portsmouth, NH: Heinemann.

Gladman, A. (2015). Team teaching is not just for teachers! Student perspectives on the collaborative classroom. *TESOL Journal, 6,* 130–148. doi:10.1002/tesj.144

Goffman, E. (1955). On face work: An analysis of ritual elements in social interaction. *Psychiatry, 18,* 213–231.

Heath, S. B., & Street, B. V. (2008). *On ethnography: Approaches to language and literacy research.* New York, NY: Teachers College Press.

Hyun, E., & Marshall, J. D. (2003). Teachable-moment-oriented curriculum practice in early childhood education. *Journal of Curriculum Studies, 35,* 111–127. doi:10.1080/00220270210125583

Martin-Beltrán, M., & Peercy, M. M. (2012). How can ESOL and mainstream teachers make the best of a standards-based curriculum in order to collaborate? *TESOL Journal, 3,* 425–444. doi:10.1002/tesj.23

Pianta, R. C., Hamre, B. K., & Mintz, S. L. (2011). *CLASS: Classroom Assessment Scoring System (manual for middle/secondary school, version 2011).* Unpublished manuscript, University of Virginia.

Valdés, G., Kibler, A., & Walqui, A. (2014). *Changes in the expertise of ESL professionals: Knowledge and action in an era of new standards.* Alexandria, VA: TESOL Press.

Wenger, E. (2009). Communities of practice: A brief introduction. Retrieved from http://www.linqed.net/media/15868/COPCommunities_of_practiceDefinedEWenger.pdf

Wilson, D., Varnhagen, S., Krupa, E., Kasprzak, S., Hunting, V., & Taylor, A. (2003). Instructors' adaptation to online graduate education in health promotion: A qualitative study. *Journal of Distance Education, 18*(2), 1–15.

Three Perspectives on TESOL Courses Told via a Learning Management System

ALSU GILMETDINOVA, LUCIANA C. DE OLIVEIRA, AND LARISA OLESOVA

The Online Course Experience

Online Courses Are "Boring"

Maria, a graduate student, has just registered for her first online course. She was cautious because of skeptical opinions she'd heard about boring online courses that are missing real class interactions. However, Maria didn't regret the decision. From the first week of classes, the course instructor and her online classmates responded to her self-introduction and asked questions about her life. This welcome drew Maria in, and she actively participated in course activities and interacted with classmates to complete weekly assignments. She received audio feedback from her course instructor on the assignment she submitted. As it turned out, her first online learning experience was great, so she couldn't understand why people express doubts about online education. Maria asked herself whether the answer is in course design or structure of assignments?

Undoubtedly, getting multiple perspectives on a course is quite valuable for students, especially to develop new knowledge and skills, apply them, and, ultimately, to have a positive learning experience in the course. This chapter acquaints readers with how a professor, a teaching assistant (TA), and a student interacted in an online TESOL education course, and how they strategically used the tools of the learning management system (LMS) to enhance each stakeholder's experience in the course.

Staking Out the Context

Online platforms that include LMSs, such as Blackboard used in this course, provide a virtual learning environment and course management system designed to guide students toward mastery of course content. The benefits of such systems have been systematically explored regarding the roles of student and teacher involvement (Klobas & McGill, 2010) and of the pedagogical, social, and technological affordances of the system (Wang, Woo, Quek, Yang, & Liu, 2012). However, much more investigation is needed to understand how the level of involvement and interaction among LMS stakeholders can support the effectiveness of a course.

In this chapter, we share our three perspectives as stakeholders who used an LMS for learning or teaching a course called English Language Development. This TESOL course is part of an English language learning licensure and certificate program offered at Purdue University in the United States. To illustrate an effective use of an LMS, we explore the integration of a student-led discussion assignment and the utilization of audio feedback. The professor and the primary instructor of the course (second author, Luciana) is an established, experienced, and progressive TESOL educator. The TA was a doctoral candidate in learning design and technology (third author, Larisa), who, among other responsibilities, was actively involved in managing the LMS. The third participant, a graduate student (first author, Alsu), was a learner taking an online course for the first time.

The Course

Philosophy and Objectives

The online course aimed at developing a wide range of skills, knowledge, and practical experience. Participants were preservice graduate students with no or limited classroom experience and practicing teachers. The course focused on understanding the literacy development of English language learners (ELLs). Course tasks stressed the importance of explicit teaching of oral and written language, the role of culture in language learning, and academic achievement, including assessment of ELLs.

Luciana took special care to foster a collaborative spirit in the online course. The course outline stated, "Collaboration with colleagues is a major part of the course, so many activities will be collaborative in nature. In addition, the instructor believes that we learn best by doing. There-fore, there will be several activities and hands-on work that will be required for the course." All the assignments mirrored this philosophy.

Theoretical Framework

Active engagement of students was a course requirement. Luciana worked with Larisa to scaffold the collaborative learning tasks to both model and teach a number of important course objec-tives. For instance, to enhance students' learning experiences they strategically built the online course environment by creating models for participants, online community-building activities, collaborative assignments, information about feedback and assessment, and active instructor/TA presence in the course (Muirhead, 2001; Wallace, 2003). This course design "challenges learners' thinking, shapes the acquisition of knowledge in meaningful ways, and changes learners, moving them toward achieving their goals" (York & Richardson, 2012, p. 84). Three out of six major course assignments were group projects. The two individual activities—participation in and leading online discussions—were intended to develop a more structured, targeted, and meaningful interaction focused on mastering and reflecting on the course content.

Among several interaction typologies that are discussed in the literature on e-learning, community of inquiry (CoI) stands out as a holistic approach to creating a meaningful learning experience. It conceptualizes interaction as a process of creating collaborative knowledge in an online learning community (Garrison, Anderson, & Archer, 2001) built around inquiry meant to challenge and intellectually engage students in online discourse. Interaction between and among students and instructors is the key element to building a dialogue and sense of connectedness in online courses.

The CoI framework consists of three overlapping elements (cognitive, teaching, and social) necessary to support higher levels of inquiry and meaningful collaboration (Garrison, Cleveland-Innes, & Fung, 2010). *Cognitive presence* is the extent to which learners construct meaning through sustained reflection and discourse. *Teaching presence* establishes the course framework to make all members realize the intended learning outcomes. *Social presence* is the ability of participants to connect and project themselves socially and emotionally within the community (Garrison & Arbaugh, 2007).

Narrative of the Classroom Interaction

Student-Led Online Discussions

This online course used a student-led approach to online discussions in which each student, as one of their posted course assignments, was responsible for leading one discussion session within their team. The first week of the semester, Luciana and Larisa modeled the process. The assignment included preparing and revising discussion questions. Next, the student discussion leader was responsible for replying to at least five postings from students by challenging, extending, and inviting peers to engage in a more in-depth examination of the readings. Last, the student moderator prepared a summary of the weekly discussion highlighting the most interesting, informative, and relevant points made by the group throughout the week.

All three elements of interaction in the CoI framework could be observed in this task. Discussion leaders could develop their cognitive presence through careful reading of the course texts with the goal of preparing questions that critiqued the readings while also inviting classmates to reflect on key ideas. Furthermore, Luciana and Larisa set high expectations for commenting on discussion posts by encouraging students to write high-quality, timely, responsive, and creative comments.

Reflections From the Student: Alsu

I decided to sign up to lead the online discussion early in the semester to have more time to perform well on it. I read the assigned texts with additional care, making many comments and highlighting thought-provoking quotes. Preparing discussion questions was not an easy task, as the objective was to elicit critical reflections and not just summaries of the readings. I revised the questions a few times At last, the questions were posted and I began closely monitoring the discussion board.

Responding to peers' posts was an eye-opening experience from multiple angles. First, I felt like an expert on the topic who needed to deepen and extend each student's idea. It was much responsibility and necessitated that I continuously went back to my notes and highlighted quotations from the readings to seek nuanced interpretations. One very important piece of advice that Luciana gave me early on was to always back up ideas with quotes.

The second discovery was that moderating the discussion took a lot of time, on average 10–15 minutes to read and comprehend the gist of a post, then 30–60 minutes to answer it: referring back to the readings, highlighting key ideas in the posts, drafting, revising, and posting the reply on blackboard.

The third novel insight was how diverse students' interpretations of the readings were. It was so unexpected to read a wide variety of perspectives on the topic. I definitely learned much from their posts. Lastly, writing the summary was quite challenging, as it required reading through all the week's posts and replies, making notes of discernable regularities and idiosyncratic ideas that provided a comprehensive answer to the discussion questions. More so, I struggled with the length of the summary, so I had to revise it multiple times to reduce it to three paragraphs.

❝ All in all, it was a great learning experience, I got much exposure to the content, felt as if I was a teacher and constantly tried to stay focused on the learning outcomes. Notably, I was able to connect with my peers through my active interaction with team members on the discussion board. ❞

Reflections From the Professor: Luciana

Giving students an opportunity to be leaders through the discussion assignment was key in implementing this type of activity online. Students were able to prepare discussion questions, and this was not always an easy task for them, as Alsu mentioned. Students sent me their questions in advance so we would negotiate what would be the best focus beyond asking about the readings for a specific week. Sometimes students struggled to come up with critical questions that went beyond the readings, but I mentored them through that process and provided some sample discussion questions. After we reached a consensus, I then posted the discussion question on Blackboard so the discussion could start. The individual student leader was responsible for reading and responding to their classmates' postings. I also replied to quite a few postings but let the student take the lead in answering questions or clarifying concepts.

This assignment helps students to feel more confident in online discussions in general, from what we observed. The assignment also addresses the three overlapping elements of the CoI framework. Students were able to construct meaning through sustained reflection and discourse (cognitive presence) as all realized the intended learning outcomes (teaching presence) through connecting and projecting themselves within the online class community (social presence).

Reflections From the Teaching Assistant: Larisa

I enjoyed my role as the TA in this online course. I had an opportunity not only to manage the online course in Blackboard but also to facilitate online discussions. For example, drawing from CoI research I prepared sample discussion questions. Then, Luciana and I chose the most helpful examples, which students used as a guide in framing their own questions.

❝ One of the positive outcomes was that students created questions at a high level of cognitive presence. They asked classmates not only to share thoughts on weekly readings but also to justify and defend their opinions in real-life situations. ❞

They shared their perspectives, discussed how their ideas could work in real classrooms and, finally, came up with a solution of how their ideas could be implemented in practice.

Next, in this course, we created groups of five to eight people and used the group tool in Blackboard for each group to carry out their online discussions. However, at the end of the semester, students asked to open the last online discussion for all students across groups. We received a very positive feedback on this initiative. Being a student in learning design and technology, I was able to apply my skills in facilitating online discussions to increase teaching and social presence. This experience was invaluable to me.

Audio Feedback

In this online course, Luciana recorded and provided audio feedback for students after they completed a case study. The case study assignment was a long-term observation of the English language development of an ELL in a classroom: at the beginning of the semester, midway through the semester, and at the end of the semester. The goal was to determine changes in the ELL's vocabulary and syntactic development in correlation to content knowledge. Each student completed a report on each of these observations. The idea to use audio feedback in this course came from Larisa and, specifically, from her dissertation topic on audio feedback.

Audio feedback in online courses is a technique in which instructors record their comments regarding students' writing assignments (Ice, 2008). The central feature of audio feedback is that it allows students to listen to previously recorded audio while they are reading instructional comments and the text to which the feedback refers (Ice, 2008). Audio feedback capabilities include establishing more personalized communication with students, enhanced online presence and student engagement, and improving overall course satisfaction (Ice, Curtis, Phillips, & Wells, 2007). Audio feedback has been shown to increase students' retention and enhance online learning community interactions. Students receiving audio feedback describe their experience as personal, enjoyable, complete, and clear (Kirschner, van den Brink, & Meester, 1991). The use of audio feedback is associated with the perception that the instructor cares in a more personal way about the student (Ice et al., 2007).

Reflections From the Student: Alsu

Audio feedback was another novel instructional technique that I experienced in this course. I was happily surprised by how easy and accessible such feedback was. All I needed to do was to open a PDF file with the rubric and double-click on the sound icon. The file momentarily opened in a new window and I could hear the instructor's voice. Listening to audio feedback enabled me to follow along with the written assignment, paying attention to the parts that Luciana was focusing on. More so, I could replay the audio many times to make sense of the feedback, to take notes about things I needed to improve for the next assignment and to hear the professor's tone. It was invaluable to be able to hear the feedback, as I could tell that she was invested in my writing, had specific commentaries, and in fact said much more than in typical written comments.

> 66 As I was listening to her voice, I felt that my assignment was important for her, that she cared about improving my knowledge and helping make my next assignment better. 99

I also appreciated listening to the feedback that Luciana gave to the entire class as I realized that my mistakes were common among several students, and I was able to get a sense of community through such feedback. All in all, audio feedback encourages students to stay intellectually engaged in not only passively receiving the feedback, but also actively making sense of it using multiple modes: listening, reading, taking notes. It also fosters developing student-instructor relationship and a sense of community.

Reflections From the Professor: Luciana

As instructors in online environments, we should use both new and established techniques to provide feedback to our students. I thought providing audio feedback would enable me to directly talk with students to make my written feedback clearer. I provided both written (comments on the margins) as well as audio feedback and felt much more connected to students by directly talking with them as if we were meeting face-to-face. This kind of feedback definitely increases the instructor's social presence in the online environment. It was also very easy to do with Audacity, which is free, open-source software for recording and editing sounds. Something different from my usual feedback processes that I did besides providing individual audio feedback was to provide what I called "overall feedback." I recorded feedback that was common across reports and made that available to all students. I first wrote down common mistakes and misunderstandings across case study reports, then ordered them by importance, then recorded my audio feedback. That really assisted students in completing their final reports. I highly recommend using audio feedback in both online and face-to-face classes.

Reflections From the Teaching Assistant: Larisa

I was introduced to audio feedback in one of my online courses, and it eventually became the topic of my dissertation. Hearing an instructional voice changed my view on teaching presence in asynchronous online environment. I had a feeling that my instructor cared about my work. Moreover, I was able to hear the tone of the voice, which made a big difference between text-based and recorded communication.

To implement audio feedback, Luciana and I had a short training session where I taught her how to record and embed feedback using Adobe Pro. Giving audio rather than text-based feedback saved her much time. Some students reported that audio feedback was more personal and easier to understand because Luciana spoke directly to each of them. Hearing a human voice with its nuances and tone in online courses generates feelings of care and belonging. It also increases the sense of presence that allows students to feel their online course instructor as a real person.

❝ This feeling of human presence behind the screen is very important in silent asynchronous online environments. ❞

In addition, the audio feedback was very effective in helping our students understand their writing gaps in order to perform better. Clear explanation is the key in text-based communication, meaning that both the tone and the format of the message are important; both need to "be relevant, responsive, accurate, and congruent with the learning task" (Bonnel, 2008, p. 292).

Conclusion

Many students who have taken online classes might be doubtful about how much content they would learn and how well they would learn it. Some might also wonder whether they would enjoy their online experience, and how they would feel along the way. Our goal in writing this chapter was to show how a meaningful and purposeful use of specific tools within Blackboard enables students to have a more positive and productive learning experience in an online TESOL class. Just like the experience of Maria that we shared in our introduction, Alsu's first online learning experience turned out to be engaging, enriching, and positive. In short, the course was intellectually stimulating because it engaged students in acquiring content-area knowledge along with the new e-learning tools. Yet, regardless of how accessible these tools were, all stakeholders—instructor, TA, and the students—needed much time to prepare. The time it takes to do online learning well must be considered by teachers who opt to design online courses and by students who decide to enroll in these courses.

Integrating various tools of LMSs in asynchronous online courses enables teachers to be more present in the course—that is, better connected with their students by serving as interactive guides as students work meaningfully through the content to accomplish course objectives. To continue offering the most up-to-date teaching methods, educators should stay abreast of novel educational technologies, and, if needed, work together with instructional designers to learn and implement the best of them in their courses. Administrators should enable these vital learning opportunities.

Lastly, building stimulating online courses depends on creating a variety of course activities, especially those geared toward group projects. Group projects help individual online participants stay connected socially and emotionally with the larger learning community. Our experience taught us that close monitoring and modeling of course expectations, as well as carefully designed assignments, are paramount for online group projects to succeed. Such successful online courses require commitment, experimentation, and a good deal of interaction among participants. Through the use of tools, such as audio feedback, we (Luciana and Larisa) were better able to connect with our students because projecting our voices created a special sense of collegiality, while our focus on clarifying tasks oriented all participants toward a high level of accomplishment.

Alsu Gilmetdinova is associate professor and director of the German-Russian Institute of Advanced Technologies at Kazan National Research Technical University named after A.N. Tupolev–KAI, Kazan, Russia.

Luciana C. de Oliveira is professor and chair of the Department of Teaching and Learning at the University of Miami, Florida, USA.

Larisa Olesova is senior instructional designer in the Office of Digital Learning at George Mason University, Fairfax, Virginia, USA.

References

Bonnel, W. (2008). Improving feedback to students in online courses. *Nursing Education Perspectives, 29*(5), 290–294.

Garrison, D. R., Anderson, T., & Archer, W. (2001). Critical thinking, cognitive presence, and computer conferencing in distance education. *American Journal of distance education, 15*(1), 7–23.

Garrison, D. R., & Arbaugh, J. B. (2007). Researching the community of inquiry framework: Review, issues, and future directions. *The Internet and Higher Education, 10*(3), 157–172.

Garrison, D. R., Cleveland-Innes, M., & Fung, T. S. (2010). Exploring causal relationships among teaching, cognitive and social presence: Student perceptions of the community of inquiry framework. *The Internet and Higher Education, 13*(1), 31–36.

Ice, P. (2008, April). *The impact of asynchronous audio feedback on teaching, social and cognitive presence.* Paper presented at the First International Conference of the Canadian Network for Innovation in Education, Banff, Alberta.

Ice, P., Curtis, R., Phillips, P., & Wells, J. (2007). Using asynchronous audio feedback to enhance teaching presence and students' sense of community. *Journal of Asynchronous Learning Networks, 11*(2), 3–25.

Kirschner, P. A., van den Brink, H., & Meester, M. (1991). Audiotape feedback for essays in distance education. *Innovative Higher Education, 15*(2), 185–195.

Klobas, J. E., & McGill, T. J. (2010). The role of involvement in learning management system success. *Journal of Computing in Higher Education, 22*(2), 114–134.

Muirhead, B. (2001). Interactivity research studies. *Journal of Educational Technology & Society, 4*(3), 108–112.

Wallace, R. M. (2003). Online learning in higher education: A review of research on interactions among teachers and students. *Education, Communication & Information, 3*(2), 241–280.

Wang, Q., Woo, H. L., Quek, C. L., Yang, Y., & Liu, M. (2012). Using the Facebook group as a learning management system: An exploratory study. *British Journal of Educational Technology, 43*(3), 428–438.

York, C. S., & Richardson, J. C. (2012). Interpersonal interaction in online learning: Experienced online instructors' perceptions of influencing factors. *Journal of Asynchronous Learning Networks, 16*(4), 83–98.

Recommendations for Online Master's in TESOL Programs: Graduate Student Voices

BURCU ATES AND KEITH M. GRAHAM

The Trend Toward Online Programs

With the advancement of technology in the last decade, online TESOL certificate and master's degree programs have increased exponentially to meet the need for quality English as a second language (ESL) and English as a foreign language (EFL) teaching around the world. The reality of many practicing English language teachers is that they may find it difficult to take time off from work to enroll in a full-time master's program (Garton & Edge, 2012). Online education potentially means anywhere and anytime learning, continued employment while studying, and continued residence (Nunan, 2012).

Because online education is a quickly expanding area in TESOL master's programs (master of arts or master of education), there is more discussion in the field about helping students navigate a master's in TESOL degree program. For example, Bagwell (2013) discussed how to choose the right program by looking at aspects such as degree name, course offerings, and type of program (face-to-face/online/hybrid) and how to evaluate a program. Murray (2013) reviewed a wide range of literature in her case report on online English language teacher education. Quality was an issue that frequently came up in that report as students worried whether online education achieved the same quality as face-to-face instruction. In his study, Prescott (2010) recommended a model for quality online TESOL training. It includes (1) learning qualities (e.g., tutor attributes [experience, promptness], feedback), (2) course structure (e.g., materials [good quality materials essential], course design [clear structure related to course objectives]), (3) technology (e.g., website [reliable, accessible]), and (4) innovation (e.g., interactive technologies [online tutorials, learning communities]). Legg and Knox (2012) also noted the importance of meaningful scaffolding activities and instructors who take time to provide written feedback to the students as well as establish a real sense of community between the students and instructors.

This chapter furthers the discussion with insights from students who have gone through an online master's in TESOL program. The first author (Burcu) is a program coordinator/academic advisor of an online master's in TESOL program and a faculty member who predominantly teaches online. Keith (second author) is a graduate of an online master's in TESOL program and an EFL teacher. In this chapter, we will share the voices of 22 graduates who completed a fully online TESOL master's degree program offered by a university in the United States. Our own experiences as an instructor and a former student and the reflections of program graduates provided us with a number of recommendations for successful online learning and teaching practices. We share these ideas in this chapter.

The Study

The context of the study was an online master's in TESOL program established in fall 2011. A variety of courses, from ESL/EFL Methodology to CALL [computer-assisted language learning] in ESL/EFL Classrooms, are offered. Study participants included 22 individuals who graduated from the program between May 2013 and August 2015. About 90% percent were teachers working while enrolled as ESL, EFL, or bilingual teachers in K–12 or university settings. The others were employees in nonteaching fields, typically seeking a career change to become ESL/EFL teachers. It is important to note that prior teaching experience is encouraged yet not a requirement of the program.

For data collection, we used an open-ended questionnaire e-mailed to participants. We sent the survey to 37 graduates, and 22 responded. Through thematic analysis, we determined the overarching themes to provide recommendations that we hope future online TESOL students and faculty will take into consideration.

Recommendations for Students

Recommendation 1: Decide Whether an Online Master's in TESOL Program is Right for You

Lisa (pseudonyms used throughout) stated, "I often find there is a misconception that online programs are easier." For those going into online learning, such a mindset could spell disaster. Therefore, before considering an online TESOL program, students should first evaluate whether the online format is right for them.

First, students need to be realistic about the time and demands an online program requires. Betsy shared,

    " Students need to be aware that an online course is just as demanding and challenging as any face-to-face course, and perhaps with the added responsibility of a full-time job and family, it becomes even more challenging. **"**

Many students choose to engage in work or other responsibilities concurrently with their online studies (Garton & Edge, 2012). In second author Keith's experience, online learning was demanding both cognitively and on his time. Keith balanced a full-time teaching job and daily foreign language classes with online degree studies. It is possible to be successful in an online program while balancing multiple responsibilities, but it requires a very clear mind about the tasks and the time required. Those who do not fully consider their time commitments are warned by Lisa that potential students could "waste their time and money" or risk "having to drop out because of the enormous demand on their time." For those considering online learning, she recommends, "being realistic about the amount of time you have to devote to it. In order to really get the most out of it, students will need at least 10–20 hours per week to devote to their studies."

In addition, students should evaluate their learning style as learning in a physical classroom differs from online learning. According to Ann, students should "expect a lot of reading and writing and become comfortable with this." Graduate study in any format inherently requires a lot of reading and writing, but this is compounded in online learning as discussions are done in written form. Those who are not comfortable with working almost exclusively with the written form and prefer oral/aural forms of interaction should consider other degree formats. In their separate accounts, both Legg and Knox (2012) discussed their struggles with the writing required of them, particularly emphasizing their discomfort with academic English and the challenges that issue created in their learning experience.

Recommendation 2: Align Your Program of Study With Your Aspirations

Once students have decided that online learning is a good fit for them, they should closely look at the offerings of different programs and find one that best matches with their interests and career aspirations. Not all TESOL master's degrees are created equal, with some degrees focusing on different aspects of the field more heavily than others. Students should consider these areas: the institution, degree name, coursework, and thesis requirements.

Beginning with the institution, prospective students should consider the university's reputation and its professors. Once students choose an institution, they should understand that TESOL master's degrees have different names that cater to different careers. Keith wanted the degree name on his diploma to highlight a certain aspect of TESOL teaching to future employers and, therefore, chose a degree that did not directly say *TESOL*. But this can be problematic at times, as April suggests:

> I feel [the title of the degree] does not accurately reflect the type of study it provides, as the content of this degree is essentially TESOL related. It tends to confuse prospective employers who are looking for those with TESOL training, and I find myself often having to explain this to others.

In terms of coursework, some students may prefer a program that leans toward ESL over EFL teaching (or vice versa) or focuses on theory-based versus practice-based study, or both. Some students may need specific courses, like Mary, who said, "There are many universities (employers) that have specific requirements for the types of classes they like to see on transcripts."

Finally, writing a master's thesis may or may not be required by a program. For those considering work in higher education, a master's thesis may be necessary. According to Mary, "Many universities overseas want their prospective instructors to have completed a thesis/capstone paper, and even have it published." For students in programs with alternative routes (e.g., action research or teaching portfolio), they may find themselves ineligible for jobs simply because they chose the wrong program. Therefore, Maria recommends that all prospective students "do careful research on their career growth requirements and credentials prior to enrolling in any program." The recommendations presented through the preceding voices align with those suggested by Bagwell (2013), who offered similar points to consider when choosing a master's program, including how to evaluate a program, which degree to choose, and the need to evaluate coursework.

Recommendation 3: Create a Time Management Plan

Once a student has enrolled in an online TESOL master's program, a major challenge will likely be time management. In the program used in this study, students are required to complete 10 courses and are encouraged to finish all coursework within 2 years. As a result of this expectation, following a schedule and studying regularly were common themes that emerged from our data set. For instance, Yolanda noted,

> The most challenging aspect of a fully online degree was time management. Being a full-time worker, full-time mom and housewife, and student made it difficult to find time to relax and breathe.

The ability to engage in self-directed learning is an obvious key to success in this learning environment. James found, "not attending regularly scheduled classes does remove the reminder to get assignments and postings in." Therefore, students should create a time management plan before the course begins. For Keith, that meant keeping a consistent schedule throughout the course, which included reading on Sunday and Monday, writing initial discussion responses and draft papers on Tuesday through Thursday, and responding to discussions and completing final drafts on Friday and Saturday. As with any plan, you need to be flexible. Maria noted, "Sometimes it takes much longer and more understanding [than anticipated] to complete assignments/projects."

Kouritzin (2002) addressed the issue of time and suggested that the online format gives students more time to think and consider ideas before sharing. Although this is clearly an advantage for deeper learning, it also requires a greater time commitment and better time management on the part of the student.

Recommendation 4: Participate in the Asynchronous Discussion Board

The asynchronous discussion board has become a common feature of online learning. For one of our participants, James, the discussion board was the reason he "learned more from classmates and professors in an online program than I ever did in a face-to-face class." However, getting the most out of a discussion board requires active participation. To get the most out of this experience, Ana recommends, "Read all of the professor and classmate comments because [students] are going to learn from each of these comments." In addition to facilitating deeper learning of course material, the discussion board can also help practicing teachers solve classroom problems. Jim shared, "If there was something I was experiencing in my teaching environment, I was able to bring that into the online discussion. Getting the feedback from others online was valuable." Students who take full advantage of the discussion board through reading and writing will, as Yolanda suggested, "gain a better understanding of various topics, whether they were from the readings, outside topics, or a personal comment from classmates."

If students or their classmates do not actively participate in online discussions, they risk losing a valuable learning experience. This situation is documented in Legg and Knox (2012) when a student, Miranda, lamented her experience in an online discussion board where her classmates did not fully participate in discussions. The lack of participation by her classmates made her feel "the discussions . . .did not tend to shape, elaborate, or deepen my understanding" (Legg & Knox, 2012, p. 55). This experience reflects those of participants in our study and shows the importance and value of being active in online discussion boards.

Recommendation 5: Find a Classroom to Apply Learning

One of the benefits of being an online TESOL master's student is you are able to continue teaching and have access to a classroom to apply course theory. For Mark, this helped develop his practice.

> I was teaching in the language classroom full-time during my master's program. Direct positive effects at the time were immediate classroom experimentation with some of the techniques I was learning as well as confirmation of some of the beliefs that I held about ELL instruction and language acquisition theory.

Like Mark, Keith often took ideas learned in the online program and immediately applied them in his classroom. This synergy helped add a layer of perspective to every theory or practice learned. A separate study of past graduates of a TESOL master's program further supports this with the finding that "the majority of participants (72%) agreed or strongly agreed that field experiences greatly enriched their courses" (Baecher, 2012, p. 585).

Although teaching while working on a TESOL master's degree potentially adds a new dimension to the learning, those without teaching experience or not working during the degree should not be discouraged. Those that do not have a classroom of their own may find it helpful to reach out to a teacher friend or classmate during the program. April recommends, "If possible, be sure you are able to spend time in a classroom on a regular basis. Find a colleague you can talk with about the things you are learning."

Recommendations for Faculty

Recommendation 1: Create an Organized Online Course

For faculty, careful organization of any course, online or face-to-face, is obviously important. However, in an online setting course design becomes especially important because when students search on their own for classroom materials and information, they need to find it easily. April stated she appreciated the planning and structure of this course by sharing her overall online experience:

> The format was clear, easy to follow, and predictable, because it was laid out in a consistent pattern which repeated itself reliably. I appreciated this very much, because with an online delivery method, it is very important for assignments, discussions, and materials to be clearly and consistently referred to and labeled, so as to avoid confusion.

Mei also acknowledged professors who "state clearly in the syllabus about the way discussion boards were designed, the requirement for assignments, and due dates for research papers." For Bruce, "professors who provided detailed calendars for due dates and explicit rubrics created an atmosphere of success despite the often rigorous coursework."

Thormann and Zimmerman (2012) argued that online instructors need to create instructional materials that are clear and to the point. For example, assignment due dates need to be clearly stated with very clear guidelines on where and when to submit.

Recommendation 2: Create Opportunities for Varied Communication and Instructional Practice

Of the participants, 10 of 22 specifically mentioned the importance of professors creating opportunities for *live* communication, and Mark recommended "more face to face communication with my classmates in terms of Skype and Google Chat." Participants disappointedly shared that live interaction was available in only a few courses. Kevin further suggested, "[a] couple of live sessions could be scheduled (morning and evening), giving students the option to join one or the other for a live lecture." Having more than one option provides the opportunity for students who are in different time zones to participate in such live sessions. Participants also wanted to see the professors' involvement in the class through voice-over PowerPoint presentations or videos to, for example, explain content. Having a PowerPoint presentation without voice or video was not considered helpful. Ann recommended, "Use as many visuals and voice-overs as possible. This helps to create a greater feeling of connection between the professor and students."

England (2012) also suggests online instructors need to provide different types of instructional materials in addition to technological tools for interaction between the instructors and students (see also Chapter 2 by Gilmetdinova, de Oliveira, & Olesova).

Recommendation 3: Be Involved in Discussion Boards

One type of comment Burcu (first author) receives repeatedly on her end-of-semester course evaluations is regarding her involvement as a professor in weekly student discussion boards. Some of her colleagues view such weekly involvement as intrusive and feel as if it imposes their own ideas on students. Burcu's experience is the contrary. For instance, April mentioned, "I really valued those times when the professors weighed-in on the discussions, as I felt it added a deeper dimension to the learning." Mary also added, "Seeing the professors participate on the discussion boards helped me as it showed that they cared about the subject matter and interacting with the students." James acknowledged the number of posts that a professor must respond to by stating, "Providing students with meaningful and constructive comments is surely a challenge." In sum, almost all participants appreciated their professor's discussion involvement.

Mandernach, Gonzales, and Garrett (2006) examined 96 online faculty members' views on participation in online course threaded discussions and found that the majority of faculty believed active participation in discussion threads were the key for an engaged online classroom.

Recommendation 4: Provide Timely Feedback to Students

Fifteen participants discussed the importance and timeliness of feedback they received from their professors. Overall, they found receiving feedback from professors extremely helpful. The quality of feedback was most important, as Mary illustrates: "Receiving critical feedback from the professors on my writing was useful and it helped me reflect on how I could improve as an educator, and as a writer." Nancy noted, "The feedback they gave for every assignment was constructive feedback and they never just said good job but also told me where I did a great job or what I needed to work on." The timeliness was appreciated, as well. Jim said, "I liked the immediate feedback" and Nancy mentioned how professors were "diligent on getting back to us as soon as possible."

Providing feedback to learners, especially emphasizing the importance of language used because online education does not have paralinguistic cues as in face-to-face interaction, is highlighted in the research literature (e.g., Murray, 2013).

Recommendation 5: Balance Theory and Practice

Another recommendation is regarding the relationship between theory and practice throughout the courses and program. Survey participants suggested that online TESOL faculty pay special attention to "a balanced approach [between practical and theoretical]" (Mary). Jim also stated, "I think the ideal TESOL program would have opportunities designed around the content to put into practice what you are learning." As we mentioned at the beginning of the chapter, about 90% of the participants in this study were practicing teachers. Understanding the theory and application was crucial to our participants' immediate needs. They have acknowledged that "it's hard for an online program to fully provide a practical approach" (April), yet we believe it is still possible through careful design of courses, selection of materials, integrated assignments, and assessments. For example, in some courses instructors supplement theoretical readings with practical handbooks that demonstrate practice in context and make the theoretical content accessible through practical explanations. Brooke had an important message to instructors:

> ❝ Provide multiple chances for application of the lessons being taught in each course. Knowing the material is all fine and well, but not being able to apply the material to the classroom makes the knowledge useless. ❞

Garton and Edge (2012) also discussed the importance of the relationship between theory and practice in their study. The responses from participants in their research illustrated clearly that theory should inform practice and practice should inform theory.

Conclusion

The recommendations we offer in this chapter emerged from the voices and reflections of graduates who have gone through the process of an online master's in TESOL program. The individual needs and preferences of the students drive their choice of program. If the decision is for online study, students need to understand their future goals and select a specific program accordingly. From the other end, instructors need to realize teaching online is not the same as teaching face-to-face. Even if they have extensive knowledge of their content and great teaching methodologies, they need to learn to incorporate these into a virtual learning environment (Murray, 2013).

For novices, the question then is *how* do I do it? Teachers can do this by participating in online teaching workshops available at their university, for instance. Or they might engage in a dialogue with other instructors who teach online and listen to the voices of students who have enrolled in online courses.

In summary, we conclude that our overall findings echo and reaffirm components of previous studies (England, 2012; Murray, 2013). In this chapter, we attempted to incorporate recent TESOL graduates' voices along with our own as part of a larger reflection about online learning from the perspectives of experienced faculty and students. Our main finding was that participants in the program wanted high-quality online TESOL training, which is rooted in a carefully designed learning environment that blends theory and practice in meaningful ways and in which instructors have significant involvement throughout.

Burcu Ates is an associate professor at Sam Houston State University, Huntsville, Texas, USA.

Keith M. Graham is a PhD student in curriculum and instruction at Texas A&M University, College Station, Texas, USA.

References

Baecher, L. (2012). Feedback from the field: What novice preK–12 ESL teachers want to tell TESOL teacher educators. *TESOL Quarterly, 46,* 578–588.

Bagwell, M. (2013). *Tips for choosing a TESOL master's program.* Retrieved from https://www.tesol .org/docs/career-center/tips-for-choosing-a-ma-in-tesol-program---michelle-bagwell-4-9-13.pdf

England, L. (Ed.). (2012). *Online language teacher education: TESOL perspectives.* New York, NY: Routledge.

Garton, S., & Edge, J. (2012). Why be an online learner in TESOL? In L. England (Ed.), *Online language teacher education: TESOL perspectives* (pp. 9–21). New York, NY: Routledge.

Kouritzin, S. G. (2002). The personal, practical, and professional rewards of teaching MA-TESOL courses online. *TESOL Quarterly, 36,* 621–624.

Legg M., & Knox, J. S. (2012). Reflections on learning TESOL at a distance. In L. England (Ed), *Online language teacher education: TESOL perspectives* (pp. 54–63). New York, NY: Routledge.

Mandernach, B. J., Gonzales, R. M., & Garrett, A. L. (2006). An examination of online instructor presence via threaded discussion participation. *MERLOT Journal of Online Learning and Teaching, 2*(4), 248–260. Retrieved from http://jolt.merlot.org/vol2no4/mandernach.htm

Murray, D. (2013). *A case for online English language teacher education.* Monterey, CA: The International Research Foundation for English Language Education. Retrieved from http://www.tirfonline.org/wp-content/uploads/2013/03/TIRF_OLTE_One-PageSpread_2013.pdf

Nunan, D. (2012). Foreword. In L. England (Ed.), *Online language teacher education: TESOL perspectives* (pp. vii–xv). New York, NY: Routledge.

Prescott, D. L. (2010). Online English language teacher training courses: Quality and innovation. *EA Journal, 26*(1), 4–40.

Thormann J., & Zimmerman, I. K. (2012). *The complete step-by-step guide to designing and teaching online courses.* New York, NY: Teachers College Press.

CHAPTER 4

General Education Teachers Discuss Their Challenges in Teaching ELLs

NILUFER GULER

The Trouble with English Language Learners

I have been teaching and counseling in-service and preservice teachers on how to teach English language learners (ELLs) at U.S. public schools for almost 10 years. During these years, I have observed that general education teachers and school administrators may have a negative perception of ELLs (an observation supported by Pettit, 2011, and Menken, 2010), and they often don't realize the distinctive role of ELL departments at schools. In fact, current research supports my observation: Though almost 42% of U.S. general education teachers need to teach ELLs, only 26.8% of U.S. teachers have had some preparation in ELL education (National Center for Educational Statistics, 2013). The negative perceptions some educators have of ELLs and ELL departments may stem from their lack of knowledge about ELL education (Pettit, 2011; Menken, 2010).

During an informal communication, an ELL coordinator of a charter school district told me that administrators at her school do not value professional development in ELL education. When I looked at the demographics of this school, I was shocked to see that ELL students composed 43% of the whole charter school's population. With little or no specialized training, teachers at this charter school (and across the United States) teach ELLs. As a result, most of the teachers perceive teaching these students as a challenge (Pettit, 2011), and some go so far as to openly state that they do not want to have ELLs in their classes (O'Brien, 2011; Reeves, 2006).

Understanding the struggles of general education teachers in teaching ELLs is crucial to help these teachers in their classrooms. There is a large body of research on how to educate these students in ELL classes, but there are far fewer studies that analyze the challenges of general education teachers in teaching ELLs (Khong & Saito, 2014). This chapter describes some of the challenges that general education teachers come across while teaching ELLs, sharing how teachers have overcome these challenges and discussing what can be done to help general education teachers better teach ELLs in their classrooms.

Researching the Issue

As a former ELL teacher and a current teacher education faculty member at a higher education institute, I wanted to understand the most common challenges that general education teachers come across while teaching ELLs and what these teachers do to overcome these challenges. To learn about these issues, I investigated two online courses: Linguistics for Educators and ESOL Practicum. Both courses were offered online at a prestigious U.S.-based university. There were 12 participants in this study: eight females and four males. All of the participants were in-service teachers.

After collecting data for one academic year, I interviewed three participants after they graduated from the program. I used three data sources for this study: participants' discussion board (DB) posts, lesson plans, and interviews. Participants did not know that their online discussions and lesson plans would be used as data for a research study while they were taking these two online classes. I decided to use student artifacts as data sources after students completed these two online courses, and I asked for their permission after the courses. All of the online student discussions and other course artifacts are original and authentic.

Findings and Discussion

Because sharing all of the challenges that participants expressed in the data is beyond the capacity of this chapter, I share only the challenges (and the sources of the challenges) that were common to all participants, both in-service and preservice teachers. The most common challenges that the teachers came across were challenges

- in finding time for differentiated instruction,
- with school administrators and other teachers, and
- in finding resources for ELLs.

Challenges in Differentiating Instruction

ELLs are usually placed in general education classes according to their grade level, and their English proficiency is ignored (Gibbons, 2014). However, ELL students in a general education classroom, even though they are at the same grade level, are not a homogenous group. They are very different in terms of their academic and language proficiency (Solano-Flores, 2008). This heterogeneity, in both non-ELLs and ELLs, causes a lot of stress for general education teachers.

On the DB, Kasey[1] described her frustration in helping her ELLs who were at different levels of proficiency:

> My next challenge is that my ELLs are advancing at different rates. Some mastered this lesson and final assessment, while others made progress but did not show mastery. So, now I have to find time to revisit these skills. I want to provide instruction within each child's Zone of Proximal Development, but I don't know how to manage that (there is only one of me!)

Kimberly had the same problem. She found it very hard to help her ELLs because their proficiency in English and their needs were often quite different.

---

[1] All names are pseudonyms.

> I still am struggling with how to help these students in the best way for each of their individual needs. I have some students that are strong in some areas and weak in others. It is hard to find lessons that will work to the best benefit of all students. I feel like I am still just stabbing in the dark at answers.

Participants found it hard to address the individual needs of their ELLs. As I was analyzing data and findings, I recognized that preservice teachers were not prepared for this diversity. I realized teacher educators should prepare their students for this challenge, and educate them on individualized lesson plans, Sheltered Instruction Observation Protocol strategies, and universal design theories.

Challenges With School Administrators and Colleagues

Participants also had several challenges related to school administrators and other general education teachers regarding educating ELLs in general education classes. Some of the teachers and administrators were biased against ELLs, or they were ignorant about the needs of these students.

Ashley thought that one of the ELLs in her classroom was not assessed correctly and she wanted her student to be tested again to see if she needed any special education services. She searched for some help to assess the academic abilities of this student better. However, Ashley felt the school administration and the ELL teacher were not very supportive.

> I realized around spring break of last year that this student was having a lot of behavior issues. After some testing, I realized this student did not even know sound-symbol relationships of many of the letters of the alphabet. I called for meetings with family, explored options for SpEd, and tried consulting with his other (our official) ELL teacher. All options lead to a dead-end and I was questioning what I was doing to advocate for him. That's when I submitted the referral. The meeting: Our head of guidance pulled my form and gave it to the ELL teacher. He "invited" me to a meeting under the guise of her wanting advice on how I get him to work for me. About 5 minutes into the meeting, I realized he called the meeting because he did not submit the form to the committee because (he said), "I think the three of us can solve this." In the course of the meeting, I realized he was not taking my professional opinion seriously and was deferring to the "professional" ELL teacher.

Larry had similar frustrations because he thought that school district administrators failed to understand the needs of ELLs and provide necessary accommodations for these students. In response to Jane's post on needing translators in some parent-teaching conferences for ELLs, Larry wrote the following post:

> One of the things that no one told me about when I became an ELL teacher was the amount of time necessary to advocate for students. At times, advocacy takes primacy over lesson planning. I have become a frequent fixture in the counseling center at my school, as I work with a counselor to find the right classes, teachers, and supports to help students for whom the system often provides not just neutral but even harmful experiences.

In addition, participants shared that their administrators wanted them, without any training, to teach ELLs, just because they had training in teaching foreign languages. When I asked Larry why he wanted to take these two online classes, he said during the interview:

> I was told by a district administrator that I would be teaching an ELL class. I had no background whatsoever, I am a French teacher, no background at all with them.

Furthermore, participants' posts had several samples of problems they encountered with principals and other teachers related to teaching ELLs. In fact, the challenges of these teachers with administrators and regular classroom teachers were concerning because of the implication that ELLs and ELL services are perceived as the "ugly step-child" (Osborne, XXXX) at the schools. This perceived difference in status led some of the participants to think that it may not be a good idea to serve as an ELL teacher after they receive their "ELL education" certificate. Corry was even worried that he would not have a close relationship with his colleagues if he chose to be an ELL teacher.

> ❝ One of the things that scares me about becoming an "ELL teacher," as opposed to a content-area teacher who works with ELLs, is that I know it's harder to be well-connected to my peers. ❞

These findings are alarming because they imply that many school administrators and general education teachers lack basic knowledge in ELL education, and they are reluctant to learn more about the subject. I believe this information adds a lot of responsibility to teacher education faculty. Teacher educators need to prepare their preservice teachers to teach and advocate for the rights of ELLs, and they should prepare several ELL education professional development opportunities for school administrators.

Challenges Finding Teaching Resources for ELLs

Participants also had a lot of challenges in finding enough appropriate sources to teach ELLs in general education classrooms. Kimberly benefited from a free magazine to teach her ELLs. It was an authentic source and it helped students to learn about the current events in the county; however, after a while she lost that resource.

> We use the newspaper, ——, which I have used as a free resource with my ELLs for many years now, but we received a letter from the company that informed us we will not receive print copies of the edition after Oct. 31, due to a lack of funding from local businesses. I have very few resources to use with my students, so this was again another blow to our school. There are other ways we can get materials, but this was a resource that I could count on to be there every day with current news and different types of stories and information available.

Participants aimed to prepare all of their students, regardless of language proficiencies, for real and academic life; however, the teaching materials they could access were not authentic—there was a mismatch between the tasks in the textbook activities and the activities the students would encounter in real life. Chris stated in Week 10 discussions that the textbook he had was not preparing his students for real life tasks and challenges.

> There was also a big difference in the level of complexity with the textbook ——, compared to the real-life map I had printed from Google maps. On the one hand, I think the scaffolding was important and necessary. On the other hand, I worry that too many textbooks over-simplify real-life activities, and give a false sense of competence. Ideally, I would have started this lesson with the textbook's simple map activities, and then finished with my real-life higher-level listening/speaking barrier activity.

This information was also eye-opening for me. I compiled a list of ELL education resources (in different formats and from different organizations and institutions) for my preservice students to help them overcome this challenge. However, even when provided with resources, teachers sometimes have a hard time distinguishing the authentic from the inauthentic and the academically appropriate from the challenging ones.

The aforementioned challenges caused teachers to feel overwhelmed and discouraged. It is very important to note that these teachers received some training in ELL education before they started to teach ELLs, yet their level of frustration was very high and they felt lost sometimes while teaching. It seems, then, that for general education teachers, teaching ELLs without any proper training in ELL education would be an overwhelming task.

How Participants Overcame Their Challenges

Participants used online discussions actively to overcome their challenges and find better ways to teach their ELLs. Sometimes they cited their problems or challenges and asked for ideas. Sometimes ideas came even before participants asked for them, and they found their classmates' posts full of helpful ideas and strategies. One student posted,

> I love the idea of bringing in different recipes. I might steal that idea for my reading class. We could write a class cookbook after we study the genre of recipes and the parts of a recipe. Hmmm . . . you really have my brain working. Thanks!

In fact, participants said that online discussions helped them so much they decided to continue these discussions after their online classes ended by starting a Facebook page:

> I cannot believe that we are nearing the end of this class. I feel so much more competent than I did last year at this time! I have really come to rely on you guys for feedback and ideas. I hope we can use our ELL Facebook page to keep our discussion going after our practicum ends.

During the interview, Ashley highlighted that her classmates' ideas and support in the DB posts helped her to have a much more professional demeanor when she interacted with her school administrators. She emphasized that she went back to the discussions several times.

> I was going through a horribly rough time with one student and the bureaucracy of our school system at the time and I remember venting in one discussion board. I went back to that board multiple times because of the support my classmates gave me. Being able to vent on the discussion board allowed me to present a more professional front to my colleagues at work and allowed me to process my beliefs . . . The practicum was designed to support my work with ELLs so I really did not feel it was a "class" as much as it was a professional development.

> 66 Yes, I learned a lot via the videos and discussion board, but the real potential, for me, was the discussion and support I received from peers. 99

DB posts and collaborative online discussions helped these general education teachers to overcome their challenges. After observing the benefits of online discussions for learning and professional development in these courses, I began to include online discussions in my graduate-level courses. Even though we meet face-to-face in class with in-service teachers, I ask them to discuss their challenges and reflect on their teachings online so that they can continue learning during the whole week and create an online community of practice with their classmates.

Implications for Developing Online Teacher Education Courses

Research shows that *all* teachers should receive some training in ELL education (O' Brien, 2011; Pettit, 2011) because ELL education requires special knowledge in different areas, and a strong pedagogical knowledge in general education is not enough (Bunch, 2013; Lucas, 2011). However, general education teachers may not have access to ELL education classes for several reasons, such as living in remote areas, busy work schedules, and family reasons. Online classes have great potential to get through to more general education teachers who wants to take classes on ELL education. This study reveals that online classes, especially online discussions, can be very effective to help general education teachers overcome their challenges related to educating ELLs in general education classes.

In her DB posts, Katie stated she changed her method of teaching several times according to her classmates' comments. DB posts and online collaborative discussions seemed to have a great impact on Katie's perception of ELL students and also on her using different teaching methods. During Week 8, she wrote the following paragraph in the DB of the Practicum class:

> I was able to take some of the suggestions you all gave me to keep the students on task. I gave them some time on Monday to share about their weekends. They were able to focus more on the lessons because they had some time to talk about other things first. I did still have to redirect on other days, but it was not as time consuming.

These online classes should be designed to include collaborative discussions and also provide opportunities for participants to reflect on their own teaching practices. This study found that online collaboration helped teachers overcome their challenges in teaching ELLs and also improved their ELL teaching methods. For example, Corry had some questions about how to teach grammar to his ELLs which resulted in a long conversation on the DB. While participants discussed the topic, they referred to course readings and other discussions. Corry referred to that particular discussion in his lesson plan and wrote the following note:

> Thanks to all of those who recommended I keep the grammar lesson functional and simple. Rather than trying to cram adverbs and adjectives in (or even call them by those names), I stuck with "modifiers" and just taught adjectives this week. I hope to keep spiraling back around each lesson to review the basics of sentence labeling and diagramming. This next week, I will teach simple question formation (flipping "subject + be" to "be + subject"). I'm eager to see how diagramming either clarifies or confuses this lesson.

In these collaborative discussions, the students shared ideas and names of some websites and books. Rob had difficulty in finding some letter and number games for his kindergarten ELLs, and he asked his classmates for ideas. Katie shared the following website with Rob to help him find more activities:

> I found this website that has more number and letter games for beginners: http://www.abcya.com/kindergarten_computers.htm
>
> Even if you don't have access to a computer lab, you could adapt some of these to off the computer. It sounds like you've had a lot of success with games, so I hope this helps.

In addition, participants used reflection as a way to observe their classroom behavior and overcome some of their differentiation-related challenges. Jane was worried that she could not differentiate her instruction for her ELLs enough; in Week 15 she wrote the following note in the reflection part of her lesson plan:

> I had worried that the ELLs would struggle with identifying the main idea in the passages, but they had more trouble with the supporting details. We talked about narrowing things down and focusing on what pertained to the main idea and that seemed to help a bit. We will be doing the same lesson later this week and I'll see if they get better at identifying the supports authors use.

While designing online classes for teachers, educators should include collaborative activities and reflections in their coursework. Both synchronous and asynchronous discussions should be part of online classes. Online classes provide learners with opportunities to put new information into practice because learners can work and study concurrently. This study found that online collaboration enhanced learning through online discussions and helped learners apply their new learning immediately. Carl had some issues in classroom management, and Corry introduced him the idea of classroom jobs. Carl could immediately use this idea; he did, and he benefitted from it.

> Oh and *Corry* thank you for the idea about the classroom jobs. I have implemented them this week and it's going great! I adapted the jobs you had, into the Caring Coach, Respectful Referee, Excellent Scorekeeper, and Super Supplier. The kids are taking ownership of their jobs and the best part is that the students are working together to ensure all of these jobs are completed! Instead of me doing all the correcting of student behavior it is the students who help remind us to be quiet or stay on task! Amazing!

The longer students interact online, the more of a rapport they build with one another. For this reason, if possible when planning an online course, teacher educators should use a cohort system so that the same group of students can take consecutive classes together. Especially at the very beginning of a course, online discussions may be superficial because of students' shyness and hesitation to share their ideas. If students get to know each other, this feeling of alienation may decrease and online discussions may be more collaborative, with students feeling more comfortable in sharing their ideas and thoughts.

Another way to help students build community, improve learning, and enhance online discussions is by including some weekly informational reading. Dewing (2012) suggests that including readings that impact emotions will also help eliminate a lack of community in online classes. During the third week of the Language for Educators course, Katie shared on the DB how the course reading helped her understand the struggles her ELLs had with pronunciation.

> One of the most significant parts of this chapter was the box that stated what English sounds people who speak other languages may struggle with. As I was reading through the list, I recognized some of the sounds that are difficult for the students in my school.

In addition, Ashley responded to another student's post and underlined how the video she watched for the Language for Educators course helped her learn more about linguistics, and this changed her thinking of how syntax needed to be taught:

> I think it was last week's video "Acquiring the Human Language" that stressed that all languages are rule governed and that there are no "primitive languages." I've been turning and turning that over in my mind. I feel this class has definitely given me a better understanding of the kinds of rules we have to teach.

Readings in a teacher education program should include theory but also include how these theories can be applied in practice (e.g., case studies).

The number of ELLs is increasing in the United States, and these students compose almost 10% of the entire U.S. public school population. ELLs lag behind their non-ELL peers in reading and math (Fry, 2008) and have a higher dropout rate than other student groups. It is crucial that we understand general education teachers' struggles and challenges in teaching ELLs. The puzzle of properly educating ELLs in U.S. public schools cannot be solved unless mainstream teachers voice their concerns and collaborate with English language specialists and empathetic administrators to determine how to best teach ELLs in their classes.

....

Nilufer Guler is an assistant professor of education at Avila University, Kansas City, Missouri, USA.

References

Bunch, G. C. (2013). Pedagogical language knowledge: Preparing mainstream teachers for English learners in the new standards era. *Review of Research in Education, 37*(1), 298–341.

Dewing, E. S. (2012). *Preparing teachers to work with English learners: Exploring the potential for transformative learning in an online English as a second language for educators' course* (Unpublished doctoral dissertation). University of Colorado, CO.

Fry, R. (2008). Role of schools in English language learner achievement gap. Retrieved from http://cf.manhattanville.edu/images/stories/Graduate_Academics_Education/ChangingSuburbs/LoHudDemographicInfo/Schools__the_ELL_Achievement_Gap.pdf

Gibbons, P. (2014). *Scaffolding language, scaffolding learning* (2nd ed.). Portsmouth, NH: Heinemann.

Khong, T. D. H., & Saito, E. (2014).Challenges confronting the teachers of English language learners. *Educational Review, 66*(2), 210–225.

Lucas, T. (2011). Language, schooling, and the preparation of teachers for linguistic diversity. In T. Lucas (Ed.), *Teacher preparation for linguistically diverse classrooms: A resource for teacher educators* (pp. 3–17). New York, NY: Routledge.

Menken, K. (2010). NCLB and English language learners: Challenges and consequences. *Theory into Practice, 49*(2), 121–128.

National Center for Education Statistics. (2013). *The condition of education 2011.* Washington, DC: U.S. Department of Education. Retrieved from http://nces.ed.gov/programs/digest/d13/tables/dt13_204.20

O'Brien, J. (2011). The system is broken and it's failing these kids: High school social studies teachers' attitudes towards training for ELLs. *The Journal of Social Studies Research, 35*(1), 22–38.

Osborne, D. (XXXX). *The ugly stepchild: On the position of ESL programs in the academy.* Manuscript submitted for publication.

Pettit, S. (2011). Teachers' beliefs of English language learners in the mainstream classroom: A review of literature. *International Multicultural Research Journal, 5*(2), 123–147.

Reeves, J. R. (2006). Secondary teacher attitudes toward including English-language learners in mainstream classrooms. *The Journal of Educational Research, 99*(3), 131–142.

Solano-Flores, G. (2008). Who is given tests in what language by whom, when, and where? The need for probabilistic views of language in the testing of English language learners. *Educational Researcher, 34*(2), 189–199.

SECTION 2:
VOICES FROM ONLINE
ESL AND EFL CONTEXTS

5 Discourse Practices of an Online Writing Tutor: A Reflective Exploration

J. ELLIOTT CASAL AND JOSEPH J. LEE

As online and blended learning environments have expanded within educational contexts, online support services such as online writing labs have emerged concurrently to provide students with additional assistance. Some online writing labs now use technologies, including audio-visual-textual conferencing (Yergeau, Wozniak, & Vandenberg, 2009), that allow tutors and student writers to engage in sustained, synchronous, one-on-one interactions. Though researchers and teacher trainers have begun to explore the processes involved in preparing teachers for online classrooms (e.g., Wang, Chen, & Levy, 2010), less attention has been paid to the training and preparation of writing tutors to be effective in digital contexts. Nonetheless, Kastman Breuch and Racine (2000) argue that "online tutors need training specific to online writing spaces" while noting the difficulty of translating training for physical spaces to digital ones in spite of the fact that learning outcomes can be "equally facilitated" in both contexts (p. 246). In this chapter, we present our reflective approach to this issue in the English Language Improvement Program (ELIP) Academic & Global Communication Program's Writing Lab at Ohio University.

The ELIP Academic & Global Communication Program's Writing Lab

As part of the Linguistics Department, the ELIP Academic & Global Communication Program, focused on academic literacies for specific purposes, offers advanced disciplinary and genre-based writing, oral communication, and critical reading instruction to matriculated first- and second-language undergraduate and graduate students. Situated within our program, the ELIP Writing Lab primarily serves student writers enrolled in ELIP courses; however, our in-person and online tutoring services are available to all members of our institution. We adopt a dialogic approach to tutoring student writers by "creating interaction-centered learning opportunities" (Walsh, 2011, p. 66). Our objective is to assist students in setting and meeting their own goals rather than evaluating or appropriating their texts.

Since our lab opened in Fall 2011, we have served approximately 170 students each semester. In Spring 2013, we began offering synchronous online tutoring to meet the needs of graduate students who were enrolled in online courses or unable to visit the physical lab for a variety of professional or personal reasons. Initially, we offered these sessions through other technologies (e.g., Google Hangouts), but currently we conduct them through WCOnline, a commonly used subscription-based scheduling system for online support services that includes a platform for online meetings. Though many technologies now allow for writing tutors and student writers to interact synchronously through audio, visual, and textual modes, we found WCOnline to be a reliable and user-friendly option. As we saw the demand for such online sessions for graduate students rise steadily over the years, we also began offering online tutoring to undergraduates.

Online sessions present our tutors with challenges that are somewhat distinct from face-to-face sessions. Among these challenges, our tutors report difficulty interacting appropriately online because the text generally occupies the center of the screen while visual dimensions of the synchronous interaction are often relegated to the periphery, as Figure 1 shows. While orienting the sessions more tightly around the text, the reduced presence of the video seems to emphasize linguistic and paralinguistic over nonverbal resources (e.g., body language). Our tutors consider this primary reliance on language to shape the interactions in these online spaces the main challenge.

At the time we conducted our exploratory inquiry, Elliott (first author) served as the lab's coordinator, and Joe (second author) was (and remains) the director of the lab. As the lab's administrators, we recognized the need to assist our tutors with their language use in online tutoring sessions. Rather than developing a top-down training system that addresses issues of tutor discourse in isolation, we began the process by critically examining online writing tutoring sessions that Elliott conducted as our first online tutor. We decided to approach this issue by engaging in a reflective exploration of Elliott's discourse practices from a series of previously recorded online tutoring sessions. Through our exploration of Elliott's discourse practices, we discovered that changes in personal discourse patterns are unlikely to occur without stimulating explicit awareness through reflective practice (Farrell, 2007; Walsh, 2011). Importantly, our goal was to develop reflective tasks for our tutors based on a better understanding of the interactions taking place in our digital lab. In the next section, we present our reflective explorations of these sessions and discuss the reflective tasks that emerged from the process.

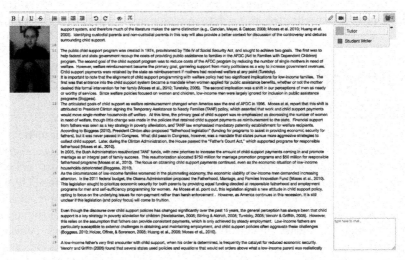

Figure 1. Illustration of an online tutoring session.

Our Reflective Exploration

Collegial Trust

We entered this project at different stages in our professional careers. Elliott recently earned his MA in linguistics and taught academic writing in various contexts, including three years at our institution. Serving as the lab's coordinator at the time, he oversaw the daily operations of the lab as well as supervised, trained, and mentored our tutors. In contrast, Joe had a PhD in applied linguistics and served as the assistant director of the ELIP Academic & Global Communication Program and director of the lab. He had been involved in applied linguistics and TESOL for nearly two decades. In Spring 2013, when these online tutoring sessions were recorded, Elliott was an MA student and served as a tutor and the assistant coordinator of the lab, and Joe was Elliott's supervisor. Since this time, we have maintained a strong professional relationship through collaboration on a number of curricular, administrative, and scholarly projects. This relationship provided an important basis of trust; Elliott had no university-level teaching experience at the time the focal tutoring sessions were recorded but was willing to revisit those sessions in Joe's presence because of this established trust.

Within this context, we decided to collaboratively explore Elliott's practices in four different hour-long online tutoring sessions he had conducted in Spring 2013 with a doctoral student, Mei (pseudonym), all of which were recorded via QuickTime's screen and audio capture functions. Focusing on linguistic and paralinguistic features impacting the tutoring process, we examined potentially missed learning opportunities during these online interactions. We followed Farrell's (2007) five-point framework for reflective practice (pp. 178–183), which serves as a set of guidelines rather than strict rules for engaging in reflective activities:

1. Provide different opportunities for reflection.

2. Build ground rules.

3. Make provisions for time.

4. Provide for external input.

5. Develop trust.

Based on these guidelines, we developed a plan of action that included both self and mediated reflective activities. For self-reflection, Elliott reviewed the recorded sessions and selected segments for further exploration in the mediated reflection meetings with Joe. In these mediated discussions, we chose to adopt modified forms of the "Speaker" and "Understander" roles defined in Edge's (1992) co-operative development framework, with Elliott as the Speaker and Joe as the Understander. The Speaker is primarily responsible for self-exploration and articulation of this reflection. The role of the Understander, according to Edge (1992), is to mediate and contribute to the Speaker's development of his or her own ideas through nonjudgmental and active listening (p. 62). However, because we consider external input to be crucially important in teacher development (Farrell, 2007), we decided against a strict application of Edge's (2002) framework. As a ground rule, we decided that Joe would primarily interact from an empathetic Understander role, but with freedom to occasionally break from the Understander role to provide input. Importantly, we adopted an approach that emphasizes "respect, empathy, and honesty" (Edge, 2002, p. 63) and trust (Farrell, 2007). Because we already had a high degree of professional familiarity and established trust, combining Edge's (2002) and Farrell's (2007) frameworks created a space for exploration, reflection, and dialogue in which we both felt safe to openly express our views. As a final note on process, the clips selected for the reflective sessions emphasize missed opportunities and, as such, are not indicative of the sessions overall.

The First Session: Articulating Assumptions

In our first meeting, we explored Elliott's assumptions, knowledge, and belief system in relation to teaching practices and tutoring practices, but also in relation to teaching online. Joe divided these issues into smaller questions, and our meeting was largely oriented around Elliott's responses. In keeping with the role of Understander in Edge's (1992) cooperative development framework, Joe listened attentively and recast Elliott's responses so that he could hear his ideas from an external perspective.

Initially, Elliott was unhappy to hear the contradictory explanations he offered. However, articulating, reformulating, and describing his beliefs regarding tutoring allowed him to move toward a more coherent image of *teacher* and *tutor*. Speaking about his practice to a colleague allowed Elliott to conceive his role as a tutor beyond a set of approaches based on experiences and officially sanctioned theories. While this interaction led to an exploration of a number of commonly used metaphors in education, Elliott emphasized his view of educators as guides. He highlighted the fact that a teacher will often *set* the destination whereas a tutor must *elicit* the destination from the student. Elliott found the act of explaining his assumptions and ideals to be challenging yet rewarding. However, as he clarified his beliefs of what an online writing tutor should be (i.e., guide), Elliott grew concerned that

> these ideas about tutoring might not surface in the actual recordings I'm about to see. I'm not sure what I will see. I expect some guiding, but I'm suddenly not sure if I'm ready to watch myself tutor on film.

The Second Session: Listening to Your Own Voice

Our second meeting focused on how Elliott's language use appeared to open or close spaces for learning. Elliott found the process to be mildly uncomfortable and selected a clip in which his language seemed to negatively impact communication in the session. Without prominent visual cues, Elliott perceived his tone as conveying a disappointed attitude at times, and some of his jokes directed to Mei struck Elliott as being harsh. In one instance, when Mei began laughing nervously as she struggled to read an overly complex sentence in her work, Elliott joined her in laughter and jokingly added "yeah, when you laugh at your own sentence. . . ." In reflection, Elliott explained,

> I was trying so hard to help her the whole time, and I wanted these talks to be fun and to show her that I was enjoying them. I was enjoying them, but sometimes I seem insensitive to the fact that she wrote all of these words.

In this case, Joe felt that it was necessary to temporarily step outside of his Understander role, something he did infrequently, to offer his interpretation. Joe agreed that some of the moments Elliott was concerned with may have negatively impacted the session, but explained that others might, in fact, be considered effective strategies within the local context of the interaction. Here, for example, Joe judged that Elliott's actions helped to bring levity to the interaction, thus reducing Mei's embarrassment. Elliott found it comforting to have his sharp self-critique moderated, but it was also useful for him to see his previous tutoring practice from an external perspective. This discussion highlighted the importance of including a trusted external agent in the reflection process.

We continued our exploration of how a tutor's communicative choices can shape the digital learning space by examining the positive impacts of providing audio cues (i.e., back-channeling) while tutees are speaking for extended periods of time. Elliott selected a clip of his interaction that showed Mei explaining her concerns while he was actively listening. Although Elliott's backchannels appeared to be excessive at first, we agreed that they seemed to positively direct the session by signaling attention and reinforcing the acceptability of an extended turn. Such signals may be difficult to transmit in a space where eye contact is limited and other forms of nonverbal communication, as previously discussed, are of reduced importance. This is one of many examples of how observing Elliott's discourse practices led to a deeper understanding of how a tutor's linguistic choices can shape online tutoring interactions.

The Third Session: Identifying Miscommunication

The third meeting underscored the difficulty of consistently teaching according to one's ideals. During mediated reflection, we reviewed a 2-minute clip in which it was clear that Mei and Elliott were not communicating effectively. After Elliott was unable to confidently identify the source of the problem, Joe helped him realize that he had strayed from the role of guide, which he had established in the first meeting. In reviewing the clip together, we noticed that Elliott had become "fixated" on a confusing aspect of Mei's text rather than attending to her priorities. In the clip, Elliott was energetic and passionate in helping her resolve an issue, but Mei demonstrated a sudden lack of interest in discussing it. In the absence of prominent nonverbal cues, Elliott persisted longer in the digital space than he likely would have in her physical presence, and Mei, rather than Elliott, conceded in the end. While he did not directly appropriate her text, such action may represent "appropriating the time" and, to a certain degree, the text indirectly. When Mei was later asked about her experiences with online tutoring, she echoed this sentiment, explaining that

" online there is a lack of spontaneity and a tendency to just focus on fixing problems, whereas in person we had more opportunities to ponder. I think you ask me more what I think and in that sense I learn more. **"**

At a personal level, it was difficult for Elliott to watch himself behave counter to his ideals, but it was a valuable reminder that we must exert continuous efforts to keep our practice consistent with our philosophy.

After exploring these issues, we discussed ways that features available in the digital environment can be used to reduce, if not avoid, such concerns. For example, participants can use chat areas to create "tutee goal lists" that remain visible throughout the session and can mark secondary concerns that arise during the session with in-text comments or highlights. Overall, our extended discussion of text appropriation yielded personal benefits for participants (e.g., awareness of personal practices) while also having broader impacts (e.g., insights for general lab practices). In this way, we began to recognize the value of our reflective activity for personal, local, and broader contexts.

The Fourth Session: Making the Best Use of the Technology

Our next meeting focused on technological aspects of training writing tutors for online tutoring. This productive session helped resolve many important technological concerns, and we explored specific practices that Mei and Elliott developed to navigate the digital space. As Elliott explained these processes, the reflective interaction shifted toward an exploration of how extensively we believed that tutors should be trained for technology use according to these specific practices. While we recognized the importance of preparing tutors with the tools to navigate the digital space, we did not want to restrict writing tutors and student writers to our processes simply because we had developed them. We agreed that it was important to, as Elliott expressed,

" balance giving the tutor the tools to make that first session work with giving the tutor and tutee together space to let the session emerge as the tutee wants or as it naturally does. **"**

Essentially, we decided that we wanted to prepare tutors for technology use while encouraging them to innovate through reflection on their own processes.

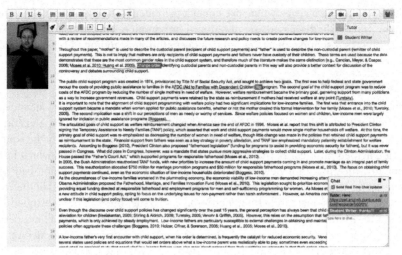

Figure 2. Illustration of tutor and tutee using chat and underline functions.

The Fifth Session: Reflecting on Training, Awareness, and Autonomy

In our final session, we explored our beliefs regarding tutor training in order to improve our approach to preparing online tutors. We agreed that training tutors for success in online spaces should include both discussion of effective discourse strategies to manage interactions with student writers and reflection on these practices to raise awareness. However, we also realized that it was crucial to maintain an atmosphere of autonomy. Figure 2 illustrates how using the chat and underline functions were common practices in one tutor-tutee relationship; in other working relationships, however, different sets of practices may develop. We wanted to reshape our training approach to provide tutors with the resources necessary to conduct sessions according to our lab's philosophies but also give them space to develop their own tutoring approach within the parameters of that philosophy. This led to a profound discussion of the relationship between the digital and physical spaces we tutored within.

Scholars debate the extent to which online and physical tutoring represents similar space and activity. However, Joe came to the conclusion that, in our context, in spite of these important differences, "we have a certain approach that we espouse to our tutors in face-to-face [sessions], and in the digital space we espouse the same thing." The realization that our goal and philosophy connect our activity in both spaces was important to us as administrators, and it has led to a more cohesive approach to training tutors for both face-to-face and online interactions.

Conclusion

In our process of improving the training we offer to online tutors, we began by reviewing online sessions Elliott had conducted. Consistent with Farrell's (2007) discussion of the "threat and associated anxiety for practicing teachers when they engage in reflective teaching" (p. 182), it was certainly not easy for Elliott, after several years of practice, to review his performance. However, in our case, the challenges were manageable, and the reflective process deepened our understanding of the digital tutoring context we shape and the interactions taking place within it. Our reflective discussions yielded a number of discoveries for us as individuals, but the significant product of this process was a series of conclusions that can inform development of reflective tasks for training in digital spaces.

First, evidence suggests that reflection can lead to a profound awareness of personal discourse practices (Farrell, 2007; Walsh, 2011). In our case, reviewing, reflecting on, and discussing Elliott's efforts to interact online according to his philosophy as a tutor has led to a deeper awareness of how interactions in online writing lab spaces can unfold. For example, our exploration of Elliott's attempt to mitigate Mei's embarrassment in Session 2 and his inconsistent attention to tonal cues in Session 3 demonstrates the importance of and challenges in effectively utilizing linguistic and paralinguistic resources in online spaces (Brummernhenrich & Jucks, 2016). It has also helped Elliott understand how his language choices can make this space suitable or unsuitable for learning.

Second, the role of and relationship with the external agent is important in engaging in reflective practice. For Elliott, the process was uncomfortable at times; it was often difficult for him to watch or listen to himself tutoring. Moreover, examining and discussing one's practices with a colleague can be even more challenging. The honesty and trust encouraged by the Speaker-Understander roles, as well as the nature of our professional relationship, were crucial in this endeavor. Success required Elliott to be open to criticism and for Joe to be a patient and empathetic listener. At the same time, on more than one occasion, Joe's expertise and knowledge helped drive Elliott's reflection toward deeper understanding. This demonstrated how the external agent occupies a crucial role in the process (Farrell, 2007) and must be selected with care, and how the role must be performed with great sensitivity and sincerity (see Edge, 1992, p. 63).

Third, tutors must be provided with clear, yet open, guidelines and tools necessary to reflect. Farrell's (2007) five-point plan served as an important model in our exploratory reflective activity, and we also benefited greatly from the flexibility we allowed ourselves. When sessions diverged from personal reflections to applications, we followed that lead and came to important conclusions. We recommend that reflective activities be sufficiently structured to provide direction, but open enough to allow exploration. Similarly, tutors need the tools to reflect. In our case, the first reflective meeting and the guiding hand of Joe's professional expertise provided Elliott with crucial resources and a grounded perspective that shaped his exploration of the online sessions.

In our lab, tutors preparing for online tutoring now engage in reflective conversations with trusted colleagues. They are asked to record online sessions to later reflect on with colleagues using the same nonintrusive recording methods Elliott used previously. We provide a broad framework for tutors to develop ground rules for their reflection, but allow freedom in structuring the process. At the end of each term, our tutors submit a brief narrative that summarizes their experiences and future goals.

Our reflective activity has assisted us in creating a process and space for our tutors to reflect on their online discourse practices. Furthermore, the process has allowed us to shape and share our voices within and beyond our context. This chapter represents our experiences as a narrative, which, after all, is the essence of reflection itself. Based on the benefits this exercise has yielded in our context, we highly recommend this process to other lab administrators responsible for preparing tutors for work in digital domains. We argue that online tutor training should implement reflection as an integral part of ongoing development, and this process should begin with trainers reflecting on their own online discourse practices.

J. Elliott Casal is currently a PhD student in applied linguistics at The Pennsylvania State University, State College, Pennsylvania, USA.

Joseph J. Lee, PhD, is assistant director of the ELIP Academic & Global Communication Program in the Department of Linguistics at Ohio University, Athens, Ohio, USA.

References

Brummernhenrich, B., & Jucks, J. (2016). "He shouldn't have put it that way!" How face threats and mitigation strategies affect person perception in online tutoring. *Communication Education*, *63*(3), 290–306.

Edge, J. (1992). Co-operative development. *ELT Journal*, *46*(1), 62–70.

Farrell, T. S. C. (2007). *Reflective language teaching: From research to practice*. London, United Kingdom: Continuum.

Kastman Breuch, L. M., & Racine, S. J. (2000). Developing sound tutor training for online writing centers: Creating productive peer reviewers. *Computers and Composition*, *17*(1), 245–263.

Walsh, S. (2011). *Exploring classroom discourse: Language in action*. Abingdon, United Kingdom: Routledge.

Wang, Y., Chen, N., & Levy, M. (2010). Teacher training in a synchronous cyber face-to-face classroom: Characterizing and supporting the online teachers' learning process. *Computer Assisted Language Learning*, *23*(4), 277–293.

Yergeau, M., Wozniak, K., & Vandenberg, P. (2009). Expanding the space of f2f: Writing centers and audio-visual-textual conferencing. *Kairos: A Journal of Rhetoric, Technology, and Pedagogy*, *13*(1). Retrieved from http://kairos.technorhetoric.net/13.1/topoi/yergeau-et-al

6

A Teacher's Framework for Online English for Academic Purposes Courses

HEEJIN CHANG AND SCOTT WINDEATT

Technology-Task Mismatch

The rapid growth of the internet has led to an increasing demand for online courses that can meet the needs of geographically separated audiences. These courses are frequently delivered and managed using Learning Management Systems (LMSs) such as Blackboard Learn and Moodle, which are already widely used in traditional classroom-based contexts. Teachers and course designers do not, however, always find the transition from classroom-based to online instruction straightforward. With this in mind, we investigated how teachers managed six 10-week online English for academic purposes (EAP) courses delivered using Moodle, and how teachers and learners reacted to them. We based the study on an existing framework for designing and evaluating courses. We describe this framework first and then explain how we used it to explore the experiences of learners and teachers involved in the online EAP course.

Throughout the chapter, we refer to notes from group and individual meetings with the teachers, messages from learners on Moodle discussion forums, and records showing the frequency with which each of the Moodle tools was used in designing the course task. This combined information allows us to suggest an alternative framework that matches the technology more effectively to what teachers want the language tasks to achieve. The alternative model we present here is also more effective at taking account of the users' opinions and meeting their needs.

The Framework

A number of frameworks have been proposed to guide the design of online courses, including Khan (2005), Attwell (2006), and Levy (2010), and these vary in detail and complexity. However, they are generally aimed at professional course designers, and, because of their sophistication, they are likely to require more time, experience, and commitment than most teachers have at their disposal. We therefore initially selected what we felt was the framework that was most appropriate for our context. We then elicited comments from the course designers—the teachers—and learners and examined data recorded by the LMS that was used to deliver the courses. Once we had analyzed that data, we then proposed a modified version of the framework that is more appropriate to teachers and learners who may have limited technical expertise.

Levy's (2010) framework seemed most directly applicable to the situation that many teachers find themselves in, including those in our context. He discusses the use of technology in terms of five levels:

- Level 1: *The material form*, such as the mobile phone, the digital camera, iPad

- Level 2: *Management*, relating to issues such as how the LMS is used

- Level 3: *Applications*, which is concerned with tools such as word processors, email, blogs, and videoconferencing

- Level 4: *Resources*, or authentic materials such as online newspapers and websites for language learning

- Level 5: *Components*, such as spelling and grammar checkers or electronic dictionaries.

We assumed that teachers would generally have little control over the technology that their institutions provide or their learners own. We also assumed that teachers will mostly be required to use an LMS such as Moodle or Blackboard to deliver their courses. Fortunately, however, the main components in all LMSs are likely to be quite similar. Therefore, our main concern was with Level 2, or issues that teachers face when managing learning through the LMS, and these issues generally include Levels 3 to 5 because they involve selecting and using applications, resources, and components. For example, Blackboard Learn and Moodle, LMSs which are widely used in higher education (Godwin-Jones, 2012) provide a wide variety of activities (or applications and components) and Moodle, the LMS used in our study, provides as many as 14 of these (e.g., wiki, database, glossary, forums, and external tools such as video and audio-conferencing). It was therefore important for us to understand how teachers exploit the potential of these applications and components (or their "affordances"; Gibson, 1979, and Levy, 2006) and to identify issues that teachers and learners face when using them.

To do that, we started by looking at how our teachers and learners used the EAP courses we run using Moodle. We used Levy's (2010) framework as a way of focusing on the main features of the technology that could either be useful to the users or could cause them problems. We wanted to know how the teachers manage the LMS—what activities, applications, and tools they use. We then wanted to find out how they reacted to the technology—their opinions about what was useful, what helped or caused them problems, and what they liked or disliked.

Context

The university where we conducted the study has a long history of using Moodle to deliver online and blended programs and has offered an on-campus EAP program since 2009. In 2011, the existing program was adapted to create an online version for distance or part-time learners, which allowed them, once they successfully completed the program (reaching a level equivalent to IELTS 6.0) to go on to study for an undergraduate or postgraduate degree.

The university provides three Moodle workshops for teachers, lecturers, and technical support staff: "Getting Started," "Forums and Communications," and "Quizzes."

TABLE 1. ONLINE EAP PROGRAM COURSES

LEVEL	COURSE	COURSE DESCRIPTION
EAP 1	Academic Speaking and Listening	To develop academic English speaking and listening language, skills, and strategies
EAP 1	Academic Reading and Writing	To develop academic English reading and writing language, skills, and strategies
EAP 2	Studying at University	To prepare for entry into mainstream university programs
EAP 2	Communication Processes	To enhance reading and writing in academic English
EAP 2	Academic English Skills	To improve four language skills in academic English
EAP 2	Applied Communication	To focus on academic English and academic numeracy

Online English for Academic Purposes Program Structure

The online EAP program is offered at two levels, with two courses at Level 1 (EAP 1), and four at Level 2 (EAP 2), each course lasting 10 weeks (see Table 1). Full-time learners are allowed to take all four EAP 2 courses at the same time after completing EAP 1.

Participants

Six teachers took part in the study. They had developed the online courses by adapting content from the on-campus courses in addition to other materials they sourced from the internet. They also taught the courses and were positive about the idea of using technology in their language courses and enthusiastic about learning new skills.

We also gathered data from 12 learners who had completed all six of the EAP 1 and 2 courses over a period of 20 weeks. They were from a variety of different countries (i.e., China, Egypt, India, Jordan, Japan, Korea, Thailand, United Arab Emirates) and spoke a range of languages.

Data Analysis and Results

Data included notes we took at a focus group meeting with all six of the teachers and at individual meetings with each of them, learners' discussion forum postings, emails to the teachers, and information recorded by Moodle showing which activities were used in the courses.

Comments of Learners and Teachers

Transferring experience from one medium to another.

In each of the six courses, a book format was adopted to structure the course content, using a table of contents that listed modules (like chapters) and subsections (see Figure 1).

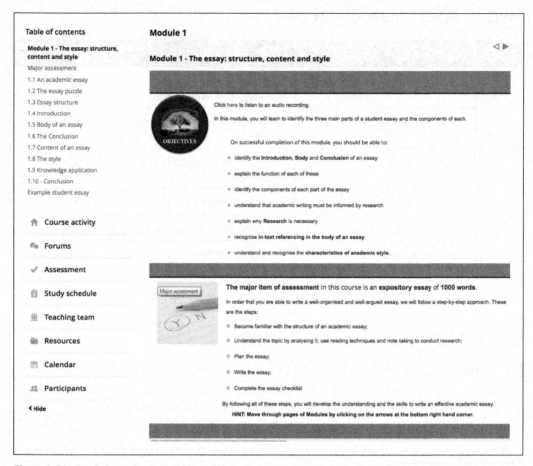

Figure 1. The book-format presentation of the course.

We expected that learners would find it straightforward to navigate through the lessons by simply selecting links to the modules and subsections from the first page of the Moodle menu. However, implementing this idea was not so straightforward. One teacher said, "It was challenging to design. . . .With the technician's advice, we used a book format. It might be easier [to navigate] if table of contents could guide them to navigate."

Learners confirmed the difficulties with navigation and functions that remained. One student said, "Actually I am not good to work with computer. I have used computer since I came to Australia, so I cannot work very good with it. Please tell me how I can find the reading in activity 1.2," and another said, "I could not access to the links for assignment 3 and I didn't know how to record. . ."

We cannot, therefore, assume that experience in one medium will transfer naturally to another medium, especially if users are struggling with the technology.

The role of technical expertise.
Teachers also encountered difficulties due to lack of experience with the technology:

> I am not tech savvy. While I am running the course, I have gone through many issues from learners and myself. At the beginning, learners had a difficulty in doing recording task because they are not familiar with uploading audio files.

Technical expertise, however, does not guarantee an understanding of how the technology can be used effectively for learning, so even when they were able to handle the technology, learners did not necessarily use the features in the way their teachers expected. According to one teacher, "[The] glossary was used for new vocabulary, but not sure of effectiveness. Simply learners seemed to copy and paste the content from online dictionaries."

The role of linguistic competence.

Apart from lack of technical expertise and limited understanding of how best to apply technology for language learning, some of the learners' technical problems stemmed from problems with the language itself, as the course was multinational. English was both the focus and the medium of learning, so it was not always clear whether problems were technical, pedagogical, or linguistic. The following problems from students appear to fall into at least two of these three categories and underline the need for clear instructions:

> I have a problem to open the link of Assignment 1: Research in the home page, whereas, I need to submit my assignment through this link. Also, I am not sure what to do for task 3 in Assignment 1.

> Hi teacher, Thank you for give me a good ideas. I have one question please. I must write outlines to support my thesis statement or can I write for example one of them against my thesis statement?

The importance of task achievement.

For the teachers, lack of technical expertise was not always perceived as a barrier to using the virtual learning environment effectively, provided they felt the features they were able to use achieved their purpose:

> 66 Honestly I don't know how to use some Moodle tools (activities). But it didn't bother me at all. The tools I use in my course work well and I am more interested in how to design task with various online sources 99

Those online sources included material available outside the LMS on the internet and were seen as providing valuable additional practice for the learners. One teacher commented, "Some learners are really poor in grammar. They need to extra work to improve their weakness. I suggested them to access the external links which developed systemically for ESL learners to learn grammar."

The difficulty in locating suitable resources.

However, finding suitable online resources was not necessarily straightforward, and teachers commented that the time and effort they spent searching for them was not always justified:

> 66 It is so hard to find proper authentic materials in reading from the web to align with module topic in the course as well as [students'] level of English. I would rather write articles for reading and examples if I have enough time to do it. 99

Another teacher said, "Providing various types of learning material and finding a proper source in online is my main concern.

Despite these problems, both teachers and learners commented positively on a number of virtual learning environment features, including the ability to provide multimedia material. One teacher said,

> . . . hoping video and audio information help them to understand the course content. I uploaded a short lecture, sometimes audio only, sometimes with video . . . Even though PPTs are mainly for on-campus learners, online learners can access them.

Student comments included,

> **❝** I like video lectures because I feel like I am attending a lecture and the teacher is talking to me. **❞**

and, "I like watching or listening lectures because it is easier to understand than to read the content only."

The importance of interaction.

Several teachers expressed a wish for more interaction between the teacher and learners with comments such as, "I would like to make it more interactive," and

> Now I have more experience of using *Moodle*. I am trying to interact more often with an individual learner by exchanging emails and providing feedback and revise and change task design to maximise learning opportunities in an online environment.

What they seemed to be referring to was not a fully developed blended learning approach, given the geographical constraints, but simply more face-to-face or one-to-one interaction. One teacher said, "I sometimes contact learners on the phone. And using Skype is helpful when learners have some issues to explore the course website." Students commented, "Thanks for a skype. Now I can access it and understand what to do," and "I was wondering could we please speak on the phone to get to know your advises in order to progress in my English level."

The benefits of online materials for different kinds of learners.

Those who benefited most from a course delivered in this way may, however, have been learners who had, or who developed, a more independent approach to learning. According to a teacher,

> **❝** Learners who enrolled the course and finished it successfully, usually were more independent and active learners. **❞**

These findings echo those of Hurd (2007). In her study of student reflections on the experience of distance learning, she found that successful distance language learning students possessed high levels of commitment and self-awareness and used different types of strategies to manage learning. However, she suggested that online language learners need support and clear instructions and feedback, and she emphasized that structured guidance is crucial.

Information Recorded by Moodle

The instructors used a range of tasks involving grammar, reading, writing, and numerical calculations, and the Moodle activities most used were Quizzes, Forums, Assignments, and Feedback. Figure 2 shows the frequency with which the activity types were used in the different courses, and Table 2 summarizes how each activity was used.

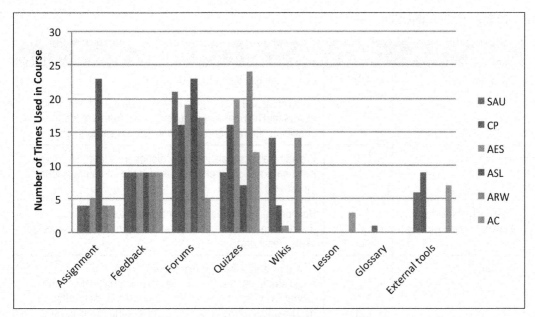

Figure 2. Moodle activities used to create a task in each of the courses. AC = Applied Communication, AES = Academic English Skills, ARW = Academic Reading and Writing, ASL = Academic Speaking and Listening, CP = Communication Processes, SAU = Studying at University.

TABLE 2. SUMMARY OF ACTIVITY USAGE

ACTIVITY	COURSES	USE
Quizzes (multiple choice, matching, short answer, numerical question types)	• AC • AES • ARW • ASL • CP • SAU	Practicing grammar, vocabulary, spelling and punctuation, and reading comprehension (Learners)
Assignment	• AC • AES • ARW • ASL • CP • SAU	Administering four assessments in each course (Teachers) In ASL, uploading audio files students had recorded (Learners)
Forums	• AC • AES • ARW • ASL • CP • SAU	Socializing and interacting with each other and teacher (Learners) Exchanging ideas, sharing opinions about course content, and making course announcements (Teachers)

Continued on next page

TABLE 2. (CONTINUED)

ACTIVITY	COURSES	USE
Wikis	• ARW • CP • AES	Encouraging collaboration (Teachers) Generating and exchanging ideas in preparation for writing essays and help for making use of notes from a reading activity in planning and writing an essay (Learners)
Glossary	• CP	Providing a personal electronic dictionary adapted from the personal notebook dictionary used in the on-campus course (Teachers)
External tools (video and audio-conferencing)	• SAU • CP • AC	Helping learners understand course content or instructions and dealing with technical issues arising from the assessment tasks (Teachers)
Resources	• AC • AES • ARW • ASL • CP • SAU	Providing audio files; providing links to external video and audio streaming files (see Figure 3) of lectures and models exemplifying how to complete given tasks; and creating documents such as PowerPoint presentations and Excel spreadsheets and charts (Teachers)

Note: AC = Applied Communication, AES = Academic English Skills, ARW = Academic Reading and Writing, ASL = Academic Speaking and Listening, CP = Communication Processes, SAU = Studying at University.

Discussion

1. How do the teachers manage the LMS? What LMS activities and other applications or tools do they use?

Of the 14 activity types available in Moodle, eight were used in the six courses. However, for the majority of tasks, teachers used only Quizzes and Forums. They used Quizzes for tasks in which automatic feedback could be provided, and Forums for more interactive tasks that required more extensive contributions from the learners or where there was no single correct answer. This finding raises the question of why so few Moodle activity types were used. Teachers may have felt that the range of language tasks they wanted to use could be satisfactorily implemented using this limited subset of the tools and that there was no pedagogical justification for using many of the other activity types. However, there was clearly a need to use a wider range of tools, because some of the learner comments related to feedback on written work, and to audio or video material, both of which could have been addressed with other tools in the Moodle suite. Some teachers and learners also suggested audio- and video-conferencing tools such as Skype, or even mobile phones.

This suggests the importance of exploring how teachers match activities to tasks and what influences the range of activities they choose to use. Biesta, Priestley, and Robinson (2015) claim that teachers' beliefs and values "play an important role" in how they "exert judgement and control over their own work" (p. 624). Influences from "the past, orientation towards the future and engagement with the present" (Biesta et al., 2015, p. 626) play an important role in pedagogical choices teachers make. We see the preference for the use of Quizzes as a reflection of teachers' beliefs, values, and past experience.

2. How do teachers and learners react to the technology?

Reactions from teachers and learners to the technology were generally positive, once initial problems had been overcome, but it is clear that the level of technological expertise varied among both teachers and learners and that this affected their reactions, especially at the start of the course. It was also clear that understanding of how materials work in one medium does not automatically transfer to another medium. Using the analogy of contents pages in printed books to facilitate navigation in the LMS, for example, did not compensate for confusion caused by lack of familiarity with the new medium in which the contents page was encountered. In addition, even learners who were comfortable with technology did not necessarily understand how certain features of the LMS could be used most effectively for language learning.

The perceived efficacy of any particular technology may be influenced by the language teachers' familiarity and experience with the technology (Levy, 2010; Godwin-Jones, 2012) and, given the initial issues that teachers reported with mastering features of the LMS, the selection or exclusion of particular Moodle activities could be linked to the teachers' perception of their ability to use those activities effectively rather than to a clear appreciation of their affordances and of their value for particular tasks. This might be because of a perceived lack of technical expertise, a lack of confidence, or a lack of time to explore a particular activity and make an informed judgment. Alternatively, there may be a mismatch between the perceived and actual affordances of the activities: They may not in practice do very effectively what they were designed to.

Conclusion: Revising Levy's (2010) Framework

In carrying out this study, we chose what we felt was an appropriate and accessible framework that could be used to help design and evaluate online courses. However, as a result of the data we gathered, we came to the conclusion that the components in this framework should be both rationalized and extended. We feel that the management of online courses and the choice of applications and components (Levy's, 2010, Levels 2, 3, and 5) are in practice likely to be linked to the issue of how much technological expertise teachers and learners have and how familiar they are with particular implementations of the technology (the applications, components, and activity types available within a particular LMS). We therefore propose that these issues should be considered as part of a single Technology category. The content of the material is clearly no less important than the technology used to deliver it, and given the difficulty that teachers may encounter in locating suitable authentic material to supplement an online course, we feel that Levy's (2010) Level 4, Resources, should be retained as our second category.

Which technology and resources should be selected may be influenced by the teacher's technological expertise and by the expectations of technologically sophisticated students. However, such choices should actually depend on the nature of the particular task. This is not accounted for in Levy's (2010) framework, and so we propose this as a new category (Task).

In addition, given the central importance of online course participants, we propose the categories of Teacher and Learner as the final two categories in our framework. Conole (2013) emphasizes that learners do not always know how to use the technologies effectively for academic work, although they may be digitally savvy. Furthermore, they are not a homogenous group; they vary in terms of their technological skills, the ways in which they use technologies, their preferences for which technologies to use, and their language proficiency level and preferred learning style. Introducing the categories of Teacher and Learner will ensure that the range of technological and pedagogical needs of users are taken into account when designing, managing, and evaluating a course. The framework we propose as a result of this study therefore consists of those five interrelated and interdependent categories: Technology, Resources, Task, Learner, and Teacher.

Perhaps the main lesson to take away from this study is the critical need to take more account of the practical issues that affect teachers and learners when providing them with new or additional technological resources. Though they can discover the potential of those resources themselves, it should not be assumed that they will have the time or the technical expertise to do so. If teachers and learners are to use a wider range of resources than they currently do—and both groups seemed keen to use other resources—administrators have to ensure that time and expertise are provided for this. At the same time, designers of learning management systems need to take notice of the fact that many of the resources and tools they provide are underused. This begs the question of whether the tools are truly fulfilling a need or need to be redesigned to make them easier to use.

Heejin Chang is a lecturer at the University of Southern Queensland, Toowoomba, Australia.

Scott Windeatt is a senior lecturer at Newcastle University, Newcastle upon Tyne, United Kingdom.

References

Attwell, G. (Ed.). (2006). *Evaluating e-learning: A guide to the evaluation of e-learning.* Bremen, Germany: Perspektiven-Offset-Druck.

Biesta, G., Priestley, M., & Robinson, S. (2015). The role of beliefs in teacher agency. *Teachers and Teaching, 21*(6), 624–640.

Conole, G. (2013). *Designing for learning in an open world.* London, England: Springer.

Gibson, J. J. (1979). The ecological approach to visual perception. Boston, MA: Houghton Mifflin.

Godwin-Jones, R. (2012). Emerging technologies challenging hegemonies in online learning. *Language Learning & Technology, 16*(2), 4–13.

Hurd, S. (2007). Anxiety and non-anxiety in a distance language learning environment: The distance factor as a modifying influence. *System, 35*(4), 487–508.

Khan, B. H. (2005). *Managing e-learning: Design, delivery, implementation and evaluation.* Hershey, PA: Information Science.

Levy, M. (2006). Effective use of CALL technologies: finding the right balance. In R. Donaldson & M. Haggstrom (Eds.), *Changing language education through CALL* (pp.1–18). New York, NY: Routledge.

Levy, M. (2010). Developing the language skills: Aligning the technological tool to the pedagogical purpose. In C. Ward (Ed.), *The impact of technology on language learning and teaching: What, how and why* (pp. 16–27). Singapore, Republic of Singapore: SEAMEO Regional Language Centre.

The Supra Tutor: Learners' Perspectives on Online Pronunciation Instruction

EDNA F. LIMA

There is no denying it: Pronunciation is a key aspect of effective oral communication. No matter how well versed an English language learner is in grammar and vocabulary, without comprehensible pronunciation, communication cannot take place successfully (Celce-Murcia & Goodwin, 1991). Poor phonemics (i.e., individual sounds) and poor control of suprasegmentals (i.e., word stress, rhythm, and intonation, which are features that extend beyond the individual sounds and are more challenging for learners to acquire) can distract the listener and hinder comprehension of the message (Eskenazi, 1999).

Although pronunciation research has become more prominent in the last few years, pronunciation teaching is still marginalized for a number of reasons. For instance, teachers lack training, support, and the ability to effectively select targets for instruction (Derwing & Munro, 2005). Moreover, instructors who venture into teaching pronunciation tend to focus heavily on "form-focused instruction (e.g., minimal pair drills) or an exclusively meaning-focused approach without explicit attention to phonological form" (Sicola & Darcy, 2015, p. 472).

My concern about pronunciation led me to create a four-module pronunciation course completely online, the Supra Tutor. In this chapter, I focus on how learners responded to the tutor, which applies a variety of pedagogical and technological applications; how they evaluated their own performance while completing the course; and how learner input may inform modifications to future iterations of this type of pronunciation teaching and learning.

Discovering Student Needs

The primary goal of the Supra Tutor was to improve the comprehensibility of international teaching assistants (ITAs) teaching at an American university in an online, self-paced environment. As one ITA pointed out,

> Sometimes my pronunciation prevents me to be understood by others. This could happen in any context.

Thus, I designed, developed, and adapted the tutor based on the needs of the ITAs taking the course. A crucial component of the Supra Tutor implementation was the administration of a needs analysis questionnaire to the ITAs to gather information about their knowledge, or lack thereof, of the suprasegmental features of English. The questionnaire served as a needs analysis instrument to inform potential changes to the tutor. Based on the survey responses, I added and altered materials as needed before the training started. For instance, given that most of the ITAs lacked training in suprasegmentals, I created additional instructional video lectures on the topics featured in the tutor. I also developed and included supplementary practice materials.

The objectives of the Supra Tutor, which drew on pedagogy and technology to offer learners an engaging and meaningful learning experience, were to help ITAs improve their comprehensibility, become aware of the suprasegmental features of American English, develop self-monitoring skills, and transfer new knowledge to novel contexts. Following is a brief description of the ITAs and of the Supra Tutor.

Twelve ITAs, seven males and five females, from a variety of fields participated in the course. The ITAs, aged from 23 to 30, were from seven different countries: Brazil, China, Ecuador, Ethiopia, India, Iran, and Jordan. On average, the ITAs had had English instruction for roughly 10 years, mostly in their home countries. Although all of them had been learning English for several years, only six had received some kind of pronunciation training, mostly at the segmental level (vowels and consonants).

The Online Tutor

The Supra Tutor (Figure 1) is a four-module fully online pronunciation course focusing on suprasegmentals (word stress, rhythm, and intonation). Each of the first three modules focuses on one given suprasegmental; the last module (review) provides ITAs with the opportunity to revisit the topics and perform additional practice activities.

I designed each module with the intention that they should be completed in a week. Modules are composed of diagnostic quizzes, instructional video lectures, perception exercises, and production exercises. The review module includes supplementary exercises and review quizzes to allow the learners to identify areas they need to revisit. The tutor includes academic and field-specific vocabulary so that learners can put what they learned into practice in academic settings. Audacity, an open-source sound editing software, and Praat, a free computer program for speech analysis, were used throughout the tutor for practice and self-monitoring. The tutor also employed scenes from TV sitcoms in perception and production exercises to engage the ITAs and to provide a diversified source of speech models. (See a tour video of the Supra Tutor at https://youtu.be/689igqyYAt8.)

Reactions to How Theory Blended With Practice

In designing and developing the Supra Tutor, I applied a variety of conceptual underpinnings. Next, I describe each of the underpinnings, including quotes from learner evaluations to illustrate how the course successfully employed these concepts.

Sequencing

Students noticed the instructional sequence I created. One ITA commented, "In this online tutor, I liked the way it is conducted. Firstly, quizzes and puzzles are given to test your knowledge. Secondly, videos and materials are provided to teach you, and finally exercises to make you strong in that area." Students appreciated that the Supra Tutor focuses on breaking down components of communication; in fact, it is based on the communicative framework for teaching pronunciation

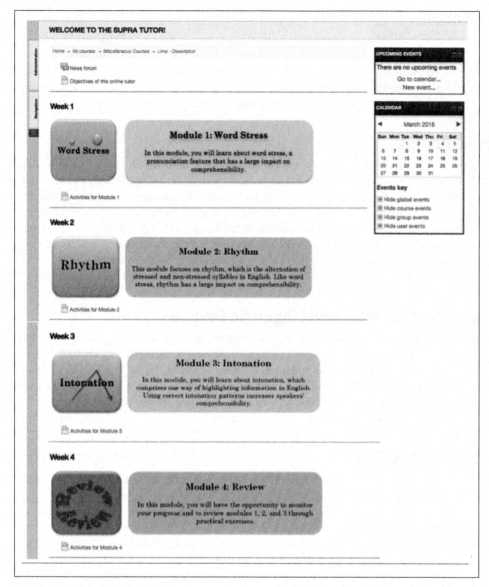

WELCOME TO THE SUPRA TUTOR!

Home → My courses → Miscellaneous Courses → Lima - Dissertation

News forum

Objectives of this online tutor

Week 1

Word Stress

Module 1: Word Stress

In this module, you will learn about word stress, a pronunciation feature that has a large impact on comprehensibility.

Activities for Module 1

Week 2

Rhythm

Module 2: Rhythm

This module focuses on rhythm, which is the alternation of stressed and non-stressed syllables in English. Like word stress, rhythm has a large impact on comprehensibility.

Activities for Module 2

Week 3

Intonation

Module 3: Intonation

In this module, you will learn about intonation, which comprises one way of highlighting information in English. Using correct intonation patterns increases speakers' comprehensibility.

Activities for Module 3

Week 4

Review

Module 4: Review

In this module, you will have the opportunity to monitor your progress and to review modules 1, 2, and 3 through practical exercises.

Activities for Module 4

UPCOMING EVENTS

There are no upcoming events

Go to calendar...
New event...

CALENDAR

◄ March 2015 ►

Sun	Mon	Tue	Wed	Thu	Fri	Sat
			1	2	3	4	5
6	7	8	9	10	11	12
13	14	15	16	17	18	19
20	21	22	23	24	25	26
27	28	29	30	31		

Events key

Hide global events
Hide course events
Hide group events
Hide user events

Figure 1. The Supra Tutor.

(Celce-Murcia, Brinton, Goodwin, & Griner, 2010, pp. 44–45). In this framework, pronunciation instruction is divided into "five phases moving from analysis and consciousness raising to listening discrimination and finally production" (p. 45). In other words, within this framework, a pronunciation lesson starts with awareness raising. This is because in second language acquisition, there is broad agreement that learners need to become aware of a given linguistic feature for learning to take place. Next, students move on to listening discrimination exercises, which include listening practice and feedback on the learner's ability to successfully recognize the feature. Next, the lesson turns to controlled practice, such as oral reading of short dialogues. After this, the lesson focuses on guided practice, which includes activities that are more structured (e.g., information-gap activities). Finally, the lesson ends with less structured activities, such as role-plays and problem-solving tasks.

Motivation

Motivation, a key goal of computer-based instructional design (Barger & Byrd, 2011), was one of the driving forces behind the development of the Supra Tutor. I designed the tutor to increase learner motivation by incorporating engaging, useful, and high-quality materials. One ITA appreciated the activities and commented that the "variety of activities and practices were definitely very useful because it made the program not boring and repeat itself as usually happens in the classroom."

Online Access

Another principle underlying my development of the Supra Tutor is online instruction. Unlike traditional face-to-face classes, online courses have the potential to offer flexibility of scheduling, individualized instruction, access to numerous speech models, a variety of cognitively oriented activities, longer practice time, and a noninhibiting learning environment. Related to these points, one ITA mentioned that, "The first and foremost benefit is flexibility of online tutor. You could work on it whenever you are free and practice." Another ITA emphasized the importance of the range of activity types, stating, "Well, the first thing [most important] is variety of activities . . . I [would] really like to go back and sing with one of those songs or watch video and repeat what they say."

Awareness of Speech and Linguistic Features

Speech awareness is also another key element behind the development of the Supra Tutor. For learners to improve, they need to become aware of their weaknesses. They also need to become aware of the linguistic features of the language. As one ITA found, "I finally understood about changes in pitch to convey information in a sentence (for example how to properly end a question sentence)." According to Chapelle (2001), "conditions directing learners' attention to linguistic form during tasks requiring meaningful language use are believed to be among the most important for learners' acquisition of target language structures" (p. 47).

Self-Monitoring

Speech awareness and awareness of linguistic features may lead to more effective self-monitoring, the last major principle guiding the development of the Supra Tutor. Self-monitoring is "a process we use to direct attention and enhance metacognitive awareness of some aspect of our cognitive and behavioral functioning" (Ellis & Zimmerman, 2001, p. 205). By monitoring their progress, learners influence their own motivation and take necessary action to acquire knowledge. For instance, an ITA stated, "I liked to hear and see (the waves) of my speech and compare it with the original words [speech model] and thus helping me to improve my performance."

Learners' Perceptions of the Supra Tutor

Quantitative Results

Upon completion of the online training, I gave the ITAs (henceforth referred to as learners) a questionnaire containing both numerical and open-ended questions in which they were asked to assess their own performance during the training. They were also prompted to evaluate the Supra Tutor in regards to usefulness, level of interest, and quality of the materials. Finally, considering that my main goal was to assess the effectiveness of fully online pronunciation instruction, I asked the learners to indicate if after the online training they would prefer to take a pronunciation course face-to-face, fully online, or half face-to-face and half online (a hybrid version). For reference in the following discussion, the 12 learners are identified as Learner 1, Learner 2, and so forth.

The questionnaire was administered online in Moodle and was included at the end of the Review module, Module 4, in the Supra Tutor.

To evaluate their own performance, the learners answered two numeric questions:

1. Before you start evaluating the materials, let's evaluate your performance. As a student during this online course, you were: 1 = extremely dedicated, 2 = dedicated, 3 = somewhat dedicated, 4 = not very dedicated, 5 = not at all dedicated.

2. As a student, I took advantage of the online materials to learn as much as I could about pronunciation, new technologies, and new learning strategies: 1 = definitely true, 2 = true, 3 = somewhat true, 4 = not at all true.

It is noteworthy that the scale I used was inverted (i.e., 1 = positive and 5 = negative) to keep consistency with other scales used in my research. For the first question, the average rating was 2.00, which indicates the learners believed they were dedicated during the online training. As for question two, the average rating was 1.41. This means the learners felt they took full advantage of the tutor to learn more about pronunciation, new technologies, and learning strategies. Figure 2 shows individual ratings for the two questions.

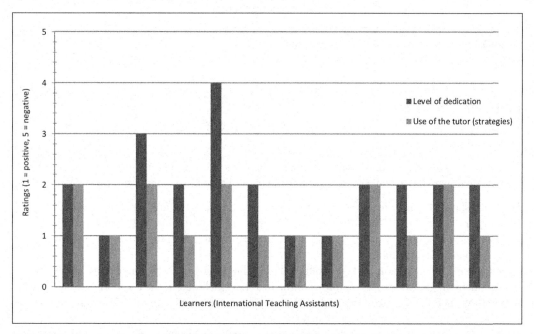

Figure 2. Learners' evaluation of their performance during the online training.

As for learner evaluation of the Supra Tutor in terms of usefulness, level of interest, and quality of the materials, the responses were positive. For usefulness, the average rating was 1.58 (1 = extremely useful, 5 = not at all useful), which indicates that the learners found the tutor to be very useful. In terms of level of interest, the average rating was 1.50 (1 = extremely interesting, 5 = not at all interesting). A rating of 1.5 means that the Supra Tutor was successful in keeping learners engaged. Finally, the tutor was perceived to be of good quality with an average rating of 1.58 (1 = excellent, 5 = poor). Figure 3 displays learners' individual assessments of the Supra Tutor.

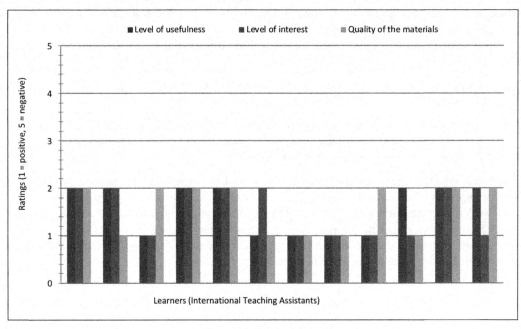

Figure 3. Learners' assessment of the Supra Tutor.

Learner Comments

Regarding usefulness, the learners commented on a variety of aspects. For instance, Learner 7 mentioned that,

❝ Due to this tutor, I am now aware of which syllable to stress and which not to. I got to know that dictionaries use symbols to indicate primary and secondary stress for words. ❞

Learner 9 stated that he liked the fact that he "was able to check the answers for the quizzes instantly and learn from it," and that "Using TV series videos to understand about American English was very useful." Learner 3 pointed out that using Audacity and Praat to "speak after the native speakers was helpful."

As part of the evaluation of the overall quality of the tutor, I included three questions in the questionnaire to gauge learners' opinions of the materials included in the tutor. They were asked to point out their favorite activities (Table 1) and their least favorite activities and to provide a brief rationale, and make suggestions for changes.

Although the learners praised the tutor in general and specifically its activities, they mentioned a few aspects they did not enjoy and suggested changes. First, several learners mentioned the crossword puzzle included after the word stress instructional lecture to check understanding. I created the puzzle as an interesting way to check their understanding of the topic. However, some of the learners found the task to be difficult and suggested that this activity be replaced. Another activity most of the learners disliked was the reading assigned for each module. They claimed that their "least favorite activity was reading the pdf files. Because, when I started reading it was very interesting but after some time I got bored" (Learner 7). Another learner mentioned that he "got too spoiled by the attractive video lectures," and that he did not want to read "boring texts" after that. All of the learners that disliked the readings suggested that they be replaced by videos

TABLE 1. LEARNERS' FAVORITE ACTIVITIES IN THE SUPRA TUTOR

LEARNER	FAVORITE SUPRA TUTOR ACTIVITIES
L1	"Recording my own sound was the most interesting part to me. For two important reasons. First, I could follow my job and see the progress. Second, I could analyze my sound and compare it with the correct one."
L2	"Introduction to the software."
L3	"I was interested in working with audacity software. Because you could listen to a conversation and then try to speak like native speakers. In this condition, if you do not know the rules you will indirectly learn like a baby. :-)"
L4	"The parts [that] include audio or video. I'm tired of any pdf lectures to learn some stuff. My performance is getting better through listening and watching."
L5	"Recording myself and analyzing the waves. I finally understood about changes in pitch to convey information in a sentence (for example how to properly end a question sentence)."
L6	"My favorite parts are doing the quiz and following your reading in audacity, really interesting. In the quiz, I found I am so bad at stress, rhythm and intonation; however, I was kind of excited. In the reading part, I heard my pronunciation is so weird, I never noticed that! Besides, I am feeling progress in the whole study procedure, which make[s] me happy."
L7	"All activities were amazing. But, my favorite activity was imitating and recording the dialogues from the different video clips. Especially, Rhythm production exercise: King of Queens: Phone number rhythm. The main reason for this being my favorite is that I never got bored, even if I record my dialogues for 100 times. This activity was fun and made me realize that, if I follow the rhythm properly while speaking, it would sound more interesting to the listener."
L8	"I liked the most the type of activity when I hear the sentence and fill in the blanks, I also liked recording the words I hear and then compare it with each other. The reason was that I liked to hear and see (the waves) of my speech and compare it with the original words and thus helped me to improve my performance."
L9	"My favorite activity in the tutor was the production exercise because I was able to apply what I have learned from the lessons, videos, and lectures."
L10	"I like them all. They are all truly interesting. And useful!"
L11	"Recording exercises. The recordings help me to visualize my pronunciation and give me a straightforward way to know my pronunciation."
L12	"Recording your [model] pronunciation because I can find my mistakes and from the comparison with the native pronunciation, I know how to change my pronunciation."

Note: L = learner.

or by a simplified version of the texts. Finally, two learners pointed out the lack of human interaction and suggested interaction with peers through a chat room or through an online meeting with me.

In terms of favored medium of instruction (face-to-face, fully online, or hybrid), none of the 12 learners chose the face-to-face option. Five learners chose fully online classes, six chose hybrid, and one learner chose both fully online and hybrid. The learner who checked both options claimed that "For me when someone goes to the regular classes they will not have the ability to extremely focus on the material, but when he has a chance he can watch the videos [online] and focus as much as he could. In addition, I chose the hybrid to make a presentation maybe for some volunteer undergrads to evaluate this TA before and after taking this course."

The learners who favored fully online pronunciation classes indicated flexibility, appealing and varied materials and activities, Praat and Audacity for practice and for speech analysis, the opportunity to revisit materials at any time, and the option to study and practice at their own pace to be key features. Learner 7 stated, "This tutor is very amazing and it includes everything that is required to teach pronunciation, rhythm, intonation. Therefore, I don't feel like it should change."

Those learners who chose hybrid indicated that

66 [In a hybrid course] I get the chance to do more work online, plus have the chance to practice and ask question[s] to a professor in the meantime and when needed 99 (Learner 5)

and "I like to watch lectures and do exercises online, but I hope I can interact with instructor and peers" (Learner 11). Feedback from the instructor was another reason Learner 1 expressed his preference for a hybrid course.

Pedagogical Implications

The Supra Tutor was successful largely because it was designed based on key principles involved in computer-assisted pronunciation training: individualized instruction, opportunities for large amounts of practice, access to different speech models, self-determined pace, a noninhibiting learning setting, and the use of varied technological tools meant to enhance and facilitate the learning experience (see Celce-Murcia et al., 2010; Eskenazi, 1999; Levis, 2007; Wang & Munro, 2004). These features provide learners with opportunities that are not often possible in face-to-face instruction.

The Supra Tutor makes use of available technology including open-source software to enrich learners' experiences. Teachers do not need extensive training or a degree in educational technology to create similar activities. For instance, YouTube contains a variety of instructional videos on English pronunciation. Videos range from the path of the voice to pronunciation of individual sounds to intonational discourse. Teachers can, for example, assign videos for students to watch at home at their own pace and create practice exercises based on the videos for students to do in the classroom. By doing this, teachers can enhance the awareness-raising process and save class time for practice and feedback (flipped classroom).

Another key feature of the Supra Tutor is that it can be designed and/or adapted for any context and audience. I developed the tutor with a focus on suprasegmentals because they are more challenging for learners to acquire than segmentals (i.e., vowels and consonants). However, one could include segmental modules in the tutor to cover a broader range of pronunciation features. Teachers could, for example, easily create their own tutor version for young learners or for beginner or intermediate learners.

Another pedagogical implication of the tutor relates to its potential for teacher training. As mentioned previously, pronunciation teaching is often marginalized for a number of reasons, including teachers' lack of training and support (Derwing & Munro, 2005). The Supra Tutor could be used to train teachers and help them better understand the pronunciation features of English and to give them ideas on how to teach pronunciation effectively.

The learner perspectives voiced in this chapter reveal that, when properly conceived, online pronunciation instruction has the potential to engage learners and motivate them to continue their training. Given that this is a novel approach to pronunciation teaching, I will need to continue seeking, analyzing, and applying the feedback of users to develop and improve the Supra Tutor. My goal is to end the marginal positioning of pronunciation by providing my learners with meaningful and engaging lessons that address their individual needs and empower them to control their own learning.

Dr. Edna F. Lima is a lecturer in the English Language Improvement Program in the Linguistics Department at Ohio University, Athens, Ohio, USA.

References

Barger, A., & Byrd, K. (2011). Motivation and computer-based instructional design. *Journal of Cross-Disciplinary Perspectives in Education*, 4(1), 1–9.

Celce-Murcia, M., Brinton, D. M., Goodwin, J. M., & Griner, B. (2010). *Teaching pronunciation: A course book and reference guide* (2nd ed.). Cambridge, United Kingdom: Cambridge University Press.

Celce-Murcia, M., & Goodwin, J. M. (1991). Teaching pronunciation. In M. Celce-Murcia (Ed.), *Teaching English as a second or foreign language* (2nd ed.). Boston, MA: Heinle & Heinle.

Chapelle, C. A. (2001). *Computer application in second language acquisition: Foundations for teaching, testing and research*. Cambridge, United Kingdom: Cambridge University Press.

Derwing, T. M., & Munro, M. J. (2005). Second language accent and pronunciation teaching: A research-based approach. *TESOL Quarterly*, 39, 379–397.

Ellis, D., & Zimmerman, B. J. (2001). Enhancing self-monitoring during self-regulated learning of speech. In H. J. Hartman (Ed.), *Metacognition in learning and instruction: Theory, research and practice* (pp. 205–228). Boston, MA: Kluwer Academic.

Eskenazi, M. (1999). Using automatic speech processing for foreign language pronunciation tutoring: Some issues and a prototype. *Language Learning & Technology*, 2(2), 62–76.

Levis, J. (2007). Computer technology in teaching and researching pronunciation. *Annual Review of Applied Linguistics*, 27, 184–202.

Sicola, L., & Darcy, I. (2015). Integrating pronunciation into the language classroom. In M. Reed & J. M. Levis (Eds.), *The handbook of English pronunciation* (pp. 471–487). Malden, MA: Wiley Blackwell.

Wang, X., & Munro, M. J. (2004). Computer-based training for learning English vowel contrasts. *System*, 32(4), 539–552.

SECTION 3:
VOICES FROM HYBRID ESL AND EFL CONTEXTS

Teaching English as an International Language in Japan Through a Videoconference-Based Flipped Class

JU SEONG LEE AND YUJI NAKAMURA

New Challenges in ELT

In the past two decades or so, English language teaching (ELT) has experienced an unprecedented change in terms of the demographics of the English-speaking population: 80% of English teachers worldwide are considered to be nonnative English speakers (Canagarajah, 2006) and over 80% of English conversations occur between nonnative speakers (Crystal, 2012). As a result, multiple varieties of English (in terms of pronunciation patterns, vocabulary choices, variety of norms, etc.), such as Japanese English, Hong Kong English, and Indonesian English, have emerged and are today used for international communication. Thus, several scholars have challenged the limitations of the traditional approach to ELT in the classroom, which include methods such as presenting British and American English speakers as model English speakers and focusing predominantly on English-speaking cultures.

Given this major shift in the field of TESOL, a number of scholars have advocated for teaching English as an international language (EIL)—that is, teaching English as one language among many used in international, multilingual contexts, not teaching one particular variety of English (e.g., American English; Matsuda, 2012; McKay, 2002). Despite increasing interest in EIL, however, the literature has not fully explored relations between theory and practice (Matsuda & Friedrich, 2011). In this chapter, we explore theory and practice related to teaching EIL via a videoconference-based flipped class by connecting one university in Japan with four universities in the United States and Asian countries.

We begin our chapter with the current challenges of ELT in Japan from an EIL perspective using one private Japanese university as a case study. Next, we explore videoconferencing as a pedagogical method for implementing EIL. After that, we introduce the nature of the videoconference-based flipped class. Finally, we discuss successes and limitations of the videoconference-based flipped class and suggest possible ways to teach EIL more effectively in English as a foreign language (EFL) classrooms.

Discovery: Current Status of ELT in Japan From an English as an International Language Perspective

For many years, the Japanese government has implemented policies and initiatives related to language teaching aimed at strengthening national competitiveness. For example, the Japan Exchange and Teaching program was launched in 1987 and "a strategic plan to cultivate Japanese with English abilities" policy was implemented in 2003 with the aim of improving Japanese students' English communicative competence (Lee, 2012). Also, overseas scholarship programs for Japanese and international students along with English language programs at Japanese universities have been increasingly promoted.

Given the present sociolinguistic landscape of diverse English use and users, some Japanese scholars have raised questions about the current perceptions of internationalization and criticized current ELT in Japan for focusing predominantly on British and American English linguistic and cultural models (Honna & Takeshita, 1999; Oda, 2007; Suzuki, 2011). In Matsuda's (2003) study, a majority of Japanese English learners said they perceive English as the language of Inner Circle countries (i.e., countries in which English is the dominant language, such as the United States and United Kingdom). She observed that the linguistic and cultural stereotypes of English among Japanese learners of English might be the result of Japan's EFL textbooks and an ELT classroom approach that mainly represents U.S. and U.K. language and culture.

Challenge: Positioning of English in Professor Nakamura's Class

Ju Seong (first author) identified the aforementioned phenomenon in the spring of 2014 when he took Professor Nakamura's (Yuji, second author) course, English and English Education in Japan in the Age of Globalization, at Keio University. The aim of this class was to explore the ways globalization affects language policy and English teachers' practices. This course had 20 registered students with varying nationalities. Half of them were Japanese (including returnees), and the remaining were international students from countries such as the United States, Germany, Australia, and Singapore. Students were enrolled in a variety of majors, such as international business, law, and English literature. Students' linguistic proficiency levels varied. There were intermediate-level students (mostly Japanese students who studied in Japan up to high school) and intermediate high/advanced students (some from Expanding Circle countries, those in which English is used as a lingua franca but plays no historical or governmental role, and others from Inner Circle countries). Students from the Inner Circle tended to speak more about the content (EIL-related issues) while students from the Outer (i.e., countries in which English is used as an official language, such as Hong Kong and Singapore) and Expanding Circle countries spoke about language issues as well as the content. Even among the students from the Outer Circle countries, there was a difference in language background; for example, some students were very close to fluent levels of proficiency while others were in the center of the Outer Circle in terms of proficiency.

Over the semester, Ju Seong employed the participant observation method to interact closely with Japanese students in the natural environment (Yuji's class). His aim was to capture their perceptions toward EIL in the Japanese context (Nunan, 1992). He was often told that English in Japan is a subject to be studied to meet university entrance requirements—not a tool for communicative purposes. Also, English usage and cultural representations in Japanese English textbooks tend to mainly focus on the United Kingdom and United States. Surprisingly, a majority of Ju Seong's Japanese classmates did not know EIL nor that different varieties of Englishes exist. This finding ignited his intellectual curiosity and desire to learn more about this issue, which led him to begin a research project with Yuji.

Change: Videoconferencing as a Pedagogical Method for Teaching English as an International Language

At the end of the semester, Ju Seong talked with Yuji about the current challenge of ELT in his EFL classroom and possible pedagogical solutions. Although, according to McKay (2002), several EIL pedagogical suggestions have been made and implemented in EFL classrooms, they have been mostly limited to theoretical discussion or have encountered practical challenges. Our response was to design and implement a videoconferencing-based flipped class.

Why did we choose videoconferencing as a viable pedagogy for teaching EIL? In TESOL, several scholars have noted that both asynchronous and synchronous computer-mediated communication play positive roles in L2 language learning (e.g., enhanced motivation, more authentic interaction, reducing anxiety) in ESL and EFL classrooms (Chun, 1994). Recently, a growing number of researchers have attempted to use videoconferencing with EFL students. For example, Wu, Yen, and Marek (2011) showed that 227 Taiwanese EFL students gained confidence, increased their motivation, and improved their abilities in English through continuous videoconferencing interactions with other English users. Considering the EFL learning environment, we thought that videoconferencing could be a viable medium to expose Japanese learners of English to diverse English usages. Unlike the previous studies, which focused on enhancing English communicative competence in EFL contexts via videoconferencing, our project aimed to employ it for teaching EIL.

Our needs analysis indicated that the students were motivated to take this course for various reasons (e.g., gaining a better understanding of other varieties of English, improving English skills, deepening understanding of the role of English). To meet their expectations, we combined the pedagogical components of a flipped classroom with videoconferencing technology for teaching EIL in a Japanese EFL classroom. Our intention was to introduce the flipped classroom as a way for the students to practice problems as homework outside the classroom through asynchronous video lectures. This would create opportunities for them to engage in active group-based problem-solving activities in the classroom, while videoconferencing created an authentic and interactive learning environment (Bishop & Verleger, 2013).

Since the fall of 2014, three videoconferencing sessions have taken place synchronously by connecting four universities in the United States, Korea, Hong Kong, and Japan with Keio University in Japan. During the videoconferencing, seven ELT scholars from the United States, Japan, Korea, Hong Kong, and Indonesia spoke on TESOL-related topics in an hour-long videoconference and engaged in a Q&A discussion with Japanese students for 30 minutes. After each videoconference, we edited and uploaded it online for the videoconference-based flipped class.

This videoconference-based flipped class is unique because, unlike Bishop and Verleger's (2013) definition of the flipped classroom, Yuji operated his flipped-class both synchronously and asynchronously. That is, his students participated in a 90-minute synchronous videoconference in class followed by an asynchronous follow-up discussion in the classroom. After that, students were required to do homework related to the EIL issues. Students could watch the edited videoconference clips for their homework, and when they came back to class, they could engage in deeper discussion.

In this chapter, we focus mainly on an asynchronous videoconferencing-based flipped lesson. English teachers, language teacher educators, and even students' parents can freely access our EIL content (eslweb.wix.com/esol-roundtable) to implement a videoconferencing-based flipped lesson considering their own particular educational contexts and academic needs. A sample lesson from the asynchronous videoconference-based flipped course is provided in Appendix A.

Growth: Successes and Challenges

Voice of the Instructor

Yuji saw the results of this innovation as follows:

> I think the videoconference-based flipped class increased my students' engagement in the course material and offered exciting opportunities for creating active and interactive learning lessons. For example, I often saw my students apply content knowledge gained during the course to real-life situations as a result of the videoconference-based flipped class (e.g., interacting with the international scholars). I also saw some Japanese students, especially those with lower-intermediate English proficiency, actually use English expressions acquired from my flipped class during the group discussion.

According to Yuji, there were some educational benefits at a macrolevel.

> I think the videoconference-based flipped class also improved my traditional ELT pedagogy by creating the real-time global learning environment where my students in Japan interacted with international experts of TESOL and applied linguistics from diverse countries. From my observation, it helped broaden my students' perspectives on ELT both locally and globally, thus positively contributing to the development of informed global citizens. I think this type of flipped class could be combined and utilized for content and language integrated learning.

Yuji also cited some challenges of the videoconference-based flipped class:

> I think students from the Inner Circle (e.g., native speakers of English) tended to dominate the discussion because students from the Expanding or Outer Circle had to deal with both the content and language issues, which might have delayed their production. I received some feedback from one Japanese student about how difficult it was for ordinary Japanese students to catch up with the others (e.g., native speakers) in terms of both English speaking and listening and the content area. Next semester, I would like to come up with a new pedagogy to meet the needs of students with diverse backgrounds.

Voices From the Students

I (Ju Seong) learned through observation and discussion with students how the students perceived the videoconference-based flipped class.[1] In my notes, I state the following:

> A majority of students responded that Prof. Nakamura's class raised their awareness of EIL. For example, Oda mentioned, "I had never thought about other Englishes ever." Other students mentioned that the class gave them ample opportunities to practice speaking and writing skills. Makie, for instance, said,

> ❝ As I engaged in the discussion, I could develop communicative competence. It helped me understand diverse opinions from different professors and discuss those with my classmates. ❞

---

[1] Student names are pseudonyms.

In contrast, some participants mentioned challenges of the videoconference-based flipped class. For example, Suzuki said, "I could barely understand the different pronunciations of other Asian English speakers during the videoconference." It indicates that the students with low English proficiency levels may struggle in understanding the EIL conversation without supplementary materials, such as handouts, and additional information. Other students such as Kiyoko explained, "Background noise was the biggest barrier to understand panelists' conversation." It infers that an optimal tech-environment may help students comprehend the conversation among the participants more accurately.

Reflections on Theory and Practice

Pedagogically, we believe undergraduate EFL students in the class deepened their understanding of the content (they learned during the regular class) through this flipped practice because they could listen extensively to diverse perspectives on the topic from the ELT scholars from Inner, Outer, and Expanding Circle countries. The strength of the videoconference-based flipped class design is that it allows students to engage in a variety of activities at various points of a lesson, and it offers real-time interaction with international scholars. Through videoconferencing technology, more significantly, examples of the diversity of English used today could be shown. The scholars and students involved were mostly from the Expanding Circle countries, so the majority of the interactions were between nonnative-English-speaking users.

Although there were some positive results, there were also limitations and challenges associated with the videoconference-based flipped class. We identified technological issues, such as audio and visual breakdowns, which distracted students. One of the most critical challenges we experienced when implementing this course was a lack of pedagogical resources on EIL, so we had to create material. An outcome of this experience is that we now have a base of suitable materials for a videoconference-based flipped class.

Suggestions for Teachers: Teaching English as an International Language in EFL Classrooms

We hope this chapter can be a resource for incorporating the EIL perspective into classrooms around the world. We believe teaching EIL can help to resolve current challenges of ELT in Japan. Our chapter also highlights the potential promise of the videoconference-based flipped class.

The voices from our classroom suggest that our experience combining the topic of EIL with content and language integrated learning (CLIL) through a videoconferencing-based flipped class was successful. Unlike the dominant theoretical model of communicative language teaching, the basic principle of CLIL is to use the target language (i.e., English) as the medium of instruction in order to have an effective pathway to both advanced language proficiency and subject knowledge (Read, 2015). During the semester, Yuji connected what students heard during the panelists' talks with what students had learned from articles (e.g., Kumaravadivelu, 2001). He saw this approach as "catching three birds—communicative language teaching (e.g., speaking and listening), teaching EIL, and CLIL pedagogy—with one stone."

For colleagues interested in applying teaching EIL to online teacher education, the lesson plan in Appendix A is a starting point. First, however, teachers need to become familiar with different forms and functions of English, and this requires the availability of authentic examples and materials. There is still a lot of work to be done in this area.

This chapter represents the first step of an investigation into using a videoconferencing-based flipped classroom model. We encourage interested colleagues to do additional research about the learning outcomes of students in similar courses by addressing issues such as language abilities, para-language abilities such as attitude, and intercultural awareness.

....

Ju Seong Lee has recently defended his doctoral dissertation at the University of Illinois at Urbana-Champaign, Champaign, Illinois, USA.

Yuji Nakamura is a professor at Keio University in Tokyo, Japan.

References

Bishop, J. L., & Verleger, M. A. (2013). *The flipped classroom: A survey of the research*. Paper presented at the annual meeting of the American Society for Engineering Education, Atlanta, GA.

Canagarajah, A. S. (2006). Negotiating the local in English as a lingua franca. *Annual Review of Applied Linguistics, 26*, 197–218.

Chun, D. (1994). Using computer networking to facilitate the acquisition of interactive competence. *System, 22*(1), 17–31.

Crystal, D. (2012). *English as a global language*. Cambridge, United Kingdom: Cambridge University Press.

Honna, N., & Takeshita, Y. (1999). On Japan's propensity for native speaker English: A change in sight. *Asian Englishes, 1*(1), 117–137.

Kumaravadivelu, B. (2001). Toward a postmethod pedagogy. *TESOL Quarterly, 35*, 537–560.

Lee, H. (2012). World Englishes in a high school class: A case from Japan. In A. Matsuda (Ed.), *Principles and practices of teaching English as an international language* (pp. 154–168). Bristol, England: Multilingual Matters.

Matsuda, A. (2003). The ownership of English in Japanese secondary schools. *World Englishes, 22*(4), 483–496.

Matsuda, A. (Ed.). (2012). *Principles and practices of teaching English as an international language*. Bristol, England: Multilingual Matters.

Matsuda, A., & Friedrich, P. (2011). English as an international language: A curriculum blueprint. *World Englishes, 30*(3), 332–344.

McKay, S. L. (2002). *Teaching English as an International Language: Rethinking goals and approaches*. Oxford, England: Oxford University Press.

Nunan, D. (1992). *Research methods in language learning*. Cambridge, England: Cambridge University Press.

Oda, M. (2007). Globalization or the world in English: Is Japan ready to face the waves? *International Multilingual Research Journal, 1*(2), 119–126.

Read, J. (2015). *Assessing English proficiency for university students*. New York, NY: Palgrave Macmillan.

Suzuki, A. (2011). Introducing diversity of English into ELT: Student teachers' responses. *ELT Journal, 65*(2), 145–153.

Wu, W.-C. V., Yen, L. L., & Marek, M. (2011). Using online EFL interaction to increase confidence, motivation, and ability. *Educational Technology & Society, 14*(3), 118–129.

Appendix A: Sample Lesson

1. **Preclass Homework Assignment Questions**

   Introduce the lesson, activating students' prior knowledge by asking questions.

2. **Preclass Homework Assignment Activities**

   Play a video clip for 1 minute and check students' understanding of the discussion in terms of intelligibility and comprehensibility by asking a few prepared comprehension questions online.

3. **In-Class Activity 1: Warm-up and introduction (10 minutes)**

   Give brief answers to the aforementioned questions that take into account historical, cultural, and sociolinguistic factors of English use. Then, he or she narrows down his or her focus into EIL usage and its roles in local contexts.

4. **In-Class Activity 2: Expose students to varieties of English usage and users by playing recorded videoconferencing video clips (20 minutes)**

   Makes a transition to recorded videoconferencing video clips, which feature 20-minute panel discussion among ELT scholars.

5. **In-Class Activity 3: Small group/whole class content discussion (20 minutes)**

   Explain that this videoconference addresses important issues, such as the impacts of globalization on English language policy, English teachers' practices in the classroom, or attitudes toward EIL.

6. **In-Class Activity 4: Small group/whole class discussion: Critical reflection about English language and its users (30 minutes)**

   a. After students watch the video clip, split the class into groups of five to discuss the similarities and differences in diverse English usages and that English users encountered in the video.

   b. Ask each group to present/share their findings to the whole class.

   c. Verbally emphasize that each of speakers on the video speaks English differently by drawing attention to accents, vocabulary, idioms, sentence structure, nonverbal cues, and other linguistic features

   d. Lead the discussion to a deeper level by asking questions.

7. **Wrap-Up (10 minutes)**

   1. Present the conclusion that varieties of English are common because people of different cultures experience/think/feel/speak the same thing differently.

   2. Also emphasize that English learners/speakers in EFL contexts such as Japan do not necessary interact with native speakers of English.

   3. Finally, ask students to write up one reflective journal entry for homework.

Present, Record, and Reflect: Enhancing Presentation Skills via Carousel Poster Sessions and Mobile Videos

SEAN H. TOLAND AND DANIEL J. MILLS

Public Reading or Speaking?

In universities all over Japan, English language learners (ELLs) are required to stand in front of their classmates and deliver a presentation as part of their final grade. This appears to be a sound idea as public speaking and presentation skills are becoming increasingly important in preparing Japanese students for careers in the global economy. However, when we listened to the voices of our first- and second-year preintermediate ELLs, we heard tremendous anxiety and frustration. They were noticeably uncomfortable as they stumbled and mumbled throughout their 3-minute presentations. Afterward, the presenters inevitably encountered silence when they asked if anyone had any questions. Not only that, many students perceived the English language public speaking exercises to be pointless and culturally irrelevant. Over the years, we have heard comments such as:

- "I feel uncomfortable using my hands while speaking."

- "It's difficult to keep eye contact."

- "In Japan, we usually have to write all of our speech on the slide."

After critically reflecting on our learners' public speaking performances, we came to the conclusion that class-fronted presentations can often be nothing more than an anxiety-inducing, glorified reading, or memorization of text-heavy slides that fail to meet the intended objective of developing the students' public speaking abilities. In an effort to address this situation, we developed a seven-step metareflection model that utilizes carousel poster presentation practice sessions in conjunction with self- and peer-reflective feedback facilitated by mobile video uploaded to a learning management system (LMS). Throughout this chapter, the term *mobile video* refers to a media file created from a mobile phone or tablet. It does not include video clips recorded on a hand-held camera or laptop PC.

Mobilizing for Action

We work with approximately 25–35 preintermediate ELLs in each of our Communication and Writing classes. A significant portion of the curriculum is devoted to the development of public speaking skills. Through our action research project, we sought to examine the value of using mobile-video recordings as a reflective tool to enhance our students' presentation skills. More specifically, we wanted to know if the participants became more cognizant of elements such as eye contact, posture, gestures, voice volume, voice rhythm, and the various parts of a presentation when they viewed their public speaking performances on a smartphone screen. We investigated our students' perceptions of mobile video as it pertained to potential benefits and perceived barriers. By carefully scrutinizing our participants' perceptions of mobile-video recordings in conjunction with the underlying friction that is present in oral presentation lessons, it created an opportunity for us to establish a more engaging and nurturing learning environment that enabled our students to cultivate their public speaking competencies.

Research Questions

After searching the academic literature, our conclusion is that there isn't much published about the use of mobile-video recordings during ELLs' oral presentation classes. In this chapter, we attempt to add to the research on classroom practice and uses of technology. The project we highlight in this chapter emerged from the immediate needs of our professional practice. The following research questions guided the study:

1. What do our students perceive as potential advantages and disadvantages of the use of mobile video in an English as an international language (EIL) presentation lesson?

2. What are our students' perceptions of the self- and peer-viewing activities on the LMS?

Mobile-Assisted Language Learning

Mobile devices are portable, flexible, affordable, and highly useable (Viberg & Grönlund, 2012). Ozadamli and Uzunboylu (2015) contend that mobile learning technologies have created new learning opportunities by eliminating geographical boundaries and enabling people to learn anywhere at any time in cooperative learning environments. The flexibility that these researchers highlighted is advantageous to EIL students because they should have greater access to educational resources and authentic content, as well as more opportunities to communicate (e.g., Skype) with other language learners and native speakers.

Mobile Video: The Benefits

Video feedback has been used in foreign language acquisition research and teacher training since the early 1960s. Unedited video footage is especially beneficial in an EIL presentation lesson because the visual artifact provides learners with a more accurate version of their public speaking performances than a written evaluation or audio file (Richards & Farrell, 2005).

Gromik (2012) explained that the Japanese university participants in his study appeared to be motivated when they used mobile videos to practice their English speaking skills. In addition, he claimed that regular practice with mobile videos expanded some of the students' word counts and confidence levels. In another study that also involved Japanese EIL university students, Miles (2014) contended that learners who watched video files of their own oral presentation performance could develop greater learner autonomy via the process of self-reflection. Miles further argued that the students' sense of responsibility seemed to have been enhanced during the process of viewing their classmates' presentations. Similarly, Hensley (2009) noted that the repeated viewings of video files enhanced the objectivity of not only EIL student presenters but also their instructors and peers. Hung (2009) reported that video-enhanced reflection helped Taiwanese EIL learners' language development by fostering their information and communications technology literacy skills, "affective engagement," and "cognitive reinforcement" (p. 186). For us, the findings of these previous studies seemed promising and validated the relevance of our project.

Mobile Video: The Challenges

Although peer-review and self-reflective activities involving student-made videos have the potential to be highly beneficial learning tasks, there are a number of significant potential hazards. Videotaping a presentation can be intrusive and may result in the learners experiencing a tremendous amount of anxiety as soon as they step in front of a camera lens (Nielson & Harder, 2013) or afterward, as they watch their own image on a screen (Jordan, 2012).

Perhaps the greatest concern for educators is that of privacy. The average person stores a tremendous amount of personal data, such as text messages, photos, and video clips, on their mobile device. Mobile-assisted language learning studies in Japanese higher education settings have reported that there is a hesitancy on the part of some learners to use their mobile devices for educational purposes because of privacy concerns as well as a desire to keep their personal lives separate from their scholastic endeavors (Kondo et al., 2012; Stockwell, 2010).

In addition to being cognizant of protecting their students' privacy, educators must not disregard the various technological challenges that can confront postsecondary students required to engage in mobile learning. Technological barriers can include the affordability of up-to-date technology and the time-consuming task of providing training to students and teachers who do not possess the prerequisite skills to utilize mobile devices in the classroom.

Metareflection Model for Public Speaking

At the tertiary level, the Japanese educational system generally places a strong emphasis on assessment and passing entrance exams rather than developing communicative competencies (Kikuchi, 2013). Wroblewski et al. (2014) claimed that public speaking is considered to be "one of the most feared context-based apprehensions in Japan, even when done in Japanese" (p. 59). Our classroom experiences and the voices of our learners certainly echoed the findings of these researchers. For example, one first-year student commented: "It's not relaxing to do [a presentation]. . .I'm too nervous." Another stated: "I'm scared to do a presentation [in Japanese] in my economics seminar."

We tackled our learners' public speaking apprehension by creating a seven-step metareflection model. The seven steps of the model are completed in three 90-minute class sessions and one homework assignment. Table 1 outlines the procedure we followed.

TABLE 1. SCHEDULE FOR IMPLEMENTING THE METAREFLECTIVE MODEL

SESSION	TASKS (STEPS)	ACTIVITIES
1	Observational learning (1)	a. View model presentations
	Collaborative evaluation of videos (2)	b. Evaluate presentations in groups
2	Carousel poster presentation practice (3)	a. Lecture on the principles of visual design
		b. Create posters in computer lab
3	Carousel poster presentation practice (3)	a. Practice presentations in small groups using carousel format
	Mobile-video recording (4)	b. Record presentation with partner using mobile device
	Upload to LMS (5)	c. Upload recorded presentation to the course LMS
Assignments	Self- and peer-review activities (6)	a. Complete self- and peer-viewing activity on the course LMS
	Complete self- and peer evaluation (7)	b. Complete questionnaire (completed on the LMS)

Step 1: Observational Learning

For the initial step in the metareflection model, our learners watched two poster presentation videos. The first video highlighted a poor performance where the presenter made obvious errors, such as speaking in a barely audible voice while looking at the poster. In contrast, the second video was an inspiring showpiece, whereby the presenter spoke loudly and clearly, made eye contact, and used a variety of gestures.

Step 2: Collaborative Evaluation of Model Videos

The second step required students to watch the model videos in a small group, discuss the positive and negative elements, and evaluate each presentation. We created a 10-item evaluation sheet (Appendix A) to help guide the learners during this collaborative task.

Step 3: Carousel Poster Presentation

During the third step of the model, our students created an original poster session and presented their ideas in a carousel format. This process took place over two classes. The first class was devoted to the creation of the posters in the university's computer lab and the second to presentations. In brief, the poster sessions are a type of guided communication activity during which there are a number of short interactive person-to-person presentations going on simultaneously.

Step 4: Mobile-Video Recordings

After presenting their poster four times during the carousel activity, our students recorded their final poster presentation using personal mobile devices. To counter any issues with sound interference, each pair completed their recording session before the next group began.

Step 5: Upload Mobile Videos to LMS

In this step, we required our students to upload their presentation videos from their mobile devices to the university's LMS, which allowed the self- and peer-review activities to be conducted outside of the classroom.

Step 6: Self- and Peer-Review Activities

Without question, we believe that Step 6 is the most important element in the metareflection model. Our students were able to carefully scrutinize and critically reflect on their own presentation performance through repeated viewings. In addition, they were able to provide their peers with better quality feedback than if they had watched a classmate's presentation once in real-time.

Step 7: Complete Self- and Peer-Evaluation

The final step required our students to complete a self- and peer-evaluation sheet (Appendix A). In addition to providing a score for the presentation content and delivery, students highlighted positive aspects of the presentation they watched as well as areas they felt needed improvement.

Testing the Metareflection Model

To test students' reactions to our model, we undertook an action research project in the economics department of a private university in Japan. In our first- and second-year Communication and Writing classes, the 152 students enrolled were invited to provide feedback about the metareflection model. The response rate was 84.8%; 129 students completed the questionnaire. In addition, seven students who were purposefully recruited from one of our second-year courses took part in a focus group interview.

The survey for this study included a total of 22 questions. There were 16 Likert-scale items, two open-ended questions, and four demographic questions. The Likert-scale items were used to gauge students' perceptions toward the mobile-video viewing activities and utilized a 6-point scale, ranging from 1(strongly disagree) to 6 (strongly agree). The third part of the survey asked two open-ended questions. We included these questions to discover the participants' perceptions of the advantages and disadvantages of using mobile videos in our EIL presentation class. A native speaker of Japanese with high English proficiency translated the survey instrument into the students' first language.

Disparaging Voices From the Classroom

We were surprised to find that an overwhelming majority of the participants (88.4%) believed that mobile devices were not useful learning tools. The open-ended responses and focus group interview shed more light on this finding. One of our students reported, "I would be uncomfortable if another student looks at my pictures or texts." Whereas, another participant commented, "There is a possibility of leaking [information] to SNS. . .That would be a big problem!" These comments were not surprising, as they mirror the literature.

Most respondents (84.5%) stated that they would be uncomfortable if their presentation video was uploaded to YouTube. The majority of participants (67.1%) also indicated discomfort with posting their mobile videos on the university's LMS. These results were anticipated because many Japanese people are concerned with who has access to their online files and how that information will be used (Fife & Orjuela, 2012).

The most frequently cited disadvantage centered on the embarrassment and anxiety that occurred whenever a mobile-video record button was pressed. The students recognized their videos would be watched and scrutinized by a classmate. One student noted,

ᏻ If I do a bad presentation I will be reminded about it because there is a video. **ᏻᏻ**

Another participant commented, "If someone says my presentation was no good it would stay in my mind." These findings also tied into the literature. Horwitz, Horwitz, and Cope (1986) found that the fear of negative evaluation, test anxiety, and communication apprehension were major contributors to foreign language anxiety.

The students also had practical concerns about using their mobile devices in our classrooms. One participant stated, "It would be a big trouble if I dropped another student's iPhone. . .It would be difficult to deal with the situation." Modern mobile devices are widely touted as having a vast storage capacity, but the results from this study contradicted this widely accepted notion. The participants indicated that extra storage space on their personal mobile devices was actually quite limited because of their numerous photos, videos, game apps, and music files. One participant passionately stated, "I need some notice to prepare my phone—Tell me 1 week before! I started to record but I had to redo the presentation because my memory was full." The drain on battery power was another practical concern that emerged. One individual noted, "I had a low battery. . .I could not finish my presentation."

Encouraging Voices From the Classroom

We found that inserting a mobile device into our presentation lessons created a certain amount of stress; however, it was not an insurmountable obstacle for our students. In fact, many individuals benefited from the challenge. One participant captured this sentiment in the following manner: "Because there is a camera in front of me, I have to do a good job. . .I need to be serious when I watch my partner's video." Another one of our students commented,

ff It is easy to find points needing improvement because I can see myself objectively. **"**

That our learners could watch mobile videos more than once was considered a significant benefit. Another student captured this sentiment when she said, "I can review it repeatedly. . .I can check my presentation from different angles." Along the same lines, one student noted, "Instructors can review [my presentation] repeatedly." These statements echo the findings of Hensley (2009), who contended that watching video files more than once enhanced everyone's objectivity and Miles's (2014) belief that the self-viewing activities contributed to the development of greater learner autonomy.

The majority of our students (90.7%) agreed that mobile videos helped them improve their graded presentations. Most participants (83.7%) felt that it was helpful to have a classmate watch their presentations. All of the focus group participants were in agreement that a poster presentation format sharpened their public speaking skills in other contexts. One student commented, "Learning how to do presentations many ways is important. . .Now I can make a presentation in front of foreigners. . .[in addition,] my [Japanese language] economics class PowerPoint presentations will be better." However, six of our students felt that a "Western-style" presentation was more difficult to do. One learner stated, "I can just speak [when doing a Japanese presentation], now I need to worry about catching the audience's attention and using my hands." This comment was not surprising, because an EIL learner's confidence to speak English can be weakened by Western-style teaching practices (Cutrone, 2009). For this reason, we believe it is important to spend time in the classroom comparing cultural norms and explaining why it is sometimes necessary to adopt a Western approach when presenting to an international audience.

Conclusion

The results of this project showed us that most of our students viewed mobile-video enhanced self- and peer-reflective feedback as beneficial tools that could help them improve the quality of their EIL presentation performances. However, many students expressed concern about public speaking anxiety, the protection of personal privacy, and the cultural contrast between Western and Japanese presentation styles. Without question, we feel that incorporating mobile devices into our EIL lessons is something that required a tremendous amount of thought and careful consideration.

When we critically reflected on the first cycle of our action research project, it was painfully obvious that we had overlooked a number of important organizational and logistical issues. For example, we initially had the students record their presentations simultaneously in different parts of the classroom. Not surprisingly, 15 people talking at the same time generated a tremendous amount of noise and distorted the audio quality of the mobile videos. In subsequent cycles, we eliminated this problematic issue by having student pairs complete their recordings before allowing the next pair to begin. We also learned that it was imperative to remind students 1 week in advance to recharge their phones and make sure they had enough storage space to create a video.

This ongoing project has taught us that educators must not put the technology before the pedagogy and avoid getting stuck in the quicksand of technological determinism. Injecting a technological tool into our presentation classes did not magically transform our learners' public speaking performances into a speech given at a TED Talk. Despite the presence of a valuable learning technology, there were still some learners who did not take full advantage of this resource and failed to put in the necessary preparation before the lesson. In our postcourse discussions, we concurred that the effective use of technology in education requires sound teaching practices and the creation of a welcoming classroom environment. When these elements are aligned, technologies such as mobile videos can play an important part in improving students' skills, including their self- and peer-reflective abilities.

Sean H. Toland is an assistant professor at Nanzan University in Japan.

Daniel J. Mills is an associate professor at Ritsumeikan University in Japan.

References

Cutrone, P. (2009). Overcoming Japanese EFL learners' fear of speaking. *University of Reading: Language Studies Working Papers, 1*, 55–63.

Fife, E., & Orjuela, J. (2012). The privacy calculus: Mobile apps and user perceptions of privacy and security. *International Journal of Engineering Business Management, 5*(6), 1–10. doi:10.5772/51645

Gromik, N. A. (2012). Cell phone video recording feature as a language learning tool: A case study. *Computers & Education, 58*(1), 223–230. doi:10.1016/j.compedu.2011.06.013

Hensley, J. (2009). Using virtual portfolios to improve presentations in an EFL setting. *Journal of the Faculty of Global Communications, University of Nagasaki, 10*, 31–39.

Horwitz, E. K., Horwitz, M. B., & Cope, J. (1986). Foreign language classroom anxiety. *Modern Language Journal, 70*(2), 125–132.

Hung, H.-T. (2009). Learners' perceived value of video as mediation in foreign language learning. *Journal of Educational Multimedia and Hypermedia, 18*(2), 171–190.

Jordan, L. (2012). Video for peer feedback and reflection: Embedding mainstream engagement into learning and teaching practice. In *Research in Learning Technology Supplement: ALT-C 2012 Conference Proceedings* (pp. 16–25). Oxfordshire, England: Association for Learning Technology.

Kikuchi, K. (2013). Demotivators in the Japanese EFL context. In M. T. Apple & D. Da Silva (Eds.), *Language learning motivation in Japan* (pp. 206–224). Bristol, United Kingdom: Multilingual Matters.

Kondo, M., Ishikawa, Y., Smith, C., Sakamoto, K., Shimomura, H., & Wada, N. (2012). Mobile assisted language learning in university EFL courses in Japan: Developing attitudes and skills for self-regulated learning. *ReCALL, 24*(2), 169–187. doi:10.1017/S0958344012000055

Miles, R. (2014). The learner's perspective on assessing and evaluating their oral presentations. In M. L. Aishah, S. K. Bhatt, W. M. Chan, S. W. Chi, K. W. Chin, S. Klayklueng. . .I. Walker (Comps.), *Proceedings of CLaSIC 2014: Knowledge, Skills and Competencies in Foreign Language Education* (pp. 337–352). Singapore: NUS Centre for Language Studies.

Nielsen, B., & Harder, N. (2013). Causes of student anxiety during simulation: What the literature says. *Clinical simulation in nursing, 9*(11), e507–e512. doi:10.1016/j.ecns.2013.03.003

Ozdamli, F., & Uzunboylu, H. (2015). M-learning adequacy and perceptions of students and teachers in secondary schools. *British Journal of Educational Technology, 46*(1), 159–172. doi: 10.1111/bjet.12136

Richards, J. C., & Farrell, T. S. C. (2005). *Professional development for language teachers: Strategies for teacher learning.* New York, NY: Cambridge University Press.

Stockwell, G. (2010). Using mobile phones for vocabulary activities: Examining the effect of the platform. *Language Learning & Technology, 14*(2), 95–110.

Viberg, O., & Grönlund, Å. (2012). Mobile assisted language learning: A literature review. In M. Sprecht, M. Sharples, & J. Multisilta (Eds.), *Proceedings of the 11th International Conference on Mobile and Contextual Learning 2012* (pp. 9–16). International Association for Mobile Learning.

Wroblewski, G., Wroblewski, J., Matsumoto, T., Nozaki, I., Kamura, T., Kumashiro, R., & Shinoda, K. (2014). Factors dissuading Japanese doctors from presenting more frequently at international conferences: More than just the usual. *Journal of Medical English Education, 13*(3), 55–64.

Appendix A: Poster Presentation Evaluation Sheet

PRESENTATION CONTENT	RATING*
1. Introduction: Included greeting, name, topic, preview	1 2 3 4 5
2. Body: Talked about key points, did not read the poster or a paper	1 2 3 4 5
3. Conclusion: Included a review, thanked the listeners, asked for questions	1 2 3 4 5
4. Language/vocabulary: Effective language used, easy to understand)	1 2 3 4 5
PRESENTATION DELIVERY	
5. Posture: Speaker had good posture, looked relaxed	1 2 3 4 5
6. Gestures: Used hands to help the presentation	1 2 3 4 5
7. Eye contact: Made eye contact with the audience	1 2 3 4 5
8. Voice: Loud and clear, natural rhythm and stress	1 2 3 4 5
9. Did the presenter stand in front of the poster?	Yes / No / Sometimes
10. Did the presenter point to the poster with the wrong hand?	Yes / No / Sometimes
COMMENTS:	**SCORE:**

*1 = not present; 2 = needs extensive improvement; 3 = satisfactory; 4 = good; 5 = outstanding

CHAPTER 10

Teach Academic Reading and Writing Without Forcing Students to Read and Write: Enter the Experiential Flipped-Classroom Environment

ANDREW DOWNER AND GEORGIA DALEURE

How do we teach academic reading and writing to students without forcing them to read and write? The answer is: by not *forcing* them! We engage students in interesting and relevant activities that entice them to read to complete their tasks.

In this chapter, we focus on teaching academic reading and writing to English language learners (ELLs) who are generally not motivated to read and write. We do this by creating a stimulating environment incorporating experiential activities and introducing the flipped classroom model. The students we worked with, male students from a Gulf Cooperation Council (GCC) country, previously studied English for academic purposes in the two levels of Academic Reading and Writing, which are followed by an English for Specific Purposes course to solidify those skills in their particular background, in this case engineering.

The normal implementation strategy of the course consisted of 3 hours designated as classroom hours, and a fourth hour designated as supervised self-study, typically using Blackboard Learn to administer quizzes or supplementary practice exercises. After consulting on course development, we decided to use the fourth hour to flip the classroom. We did this by rethinking which parts of the course were best done together with the teacher and which were best done independently.

The teachers of the course overwhelmingly agreed that spending the 3 hours of class time engaging with students in authentic tasks was more important than delivering a live lecture. So, we taped the lectures and uploaded them along with supplementary activities, like quizzes and self-assessment materials. Our students could access these materials independently wherever and whenever it best suited them. This flip opened up our lessons so that we could spend time in class working on language production.

Curriculum Objectives

The English for Specific Purposes: Engineering Technology course prepares future engineers at our institution to write technical reports and make effective English presentations. To fulfill the learning outcomes of the course, students must research a theoretical concept (showing evidence of reading), describe the process of testing the concept, analyze their results, interpret their findings, and reflect on their learning experience. Students produce a written report and an audiovisual presentation. The course is designed to prepare students for undertaking their final year capstone projects.

Pedagogic Approach

Experiential Learning

Experiential learning, one form of which is the flipped classroom model, has been termed *learning by doing* because it shifts class activities from rote learning to active learning procedures (Dale, 1969). Assessments are based on achieving milestones set by industry leading to the construction of learning environments that are as authentic as possible; therefore, experiential learning is a great option for introducing content to students studying in their nonnative language (Raddawi, 2012).

Flipped Classroom and Blended Learning

The flipped classroom experience, according to Bishop and Verleger (2013), "is a new pedagogical method, which employs asynchronous video lectures and practice problems as homework, and active, group-based problem solving activities in the classroom" (p. 2). The authors further emphasize that, "the flipped classroom actually represents an expansion of the curriculum, rather than a mere re-arrangement of activities (utilizing) interactive group learning activities inside the classroom and direct computer-based individual instruction outside the classroom" (p. 4).

In the flipped TESOL model, instructional sessions are recorded and assigned as homework before the lesson. The input is usually geared to introduce vocabulary, grammar, or other concepts that can be easily and clearly demonstrated by the use of videos, online quizzes, and other activities. The online activities prepare students to work through higher order learning tasks in the classroom with teacher. In the class, the learning activities are extended and students continue to build on previous learning by engaging in higher level learning activities in the class individually or in groups with the teacher. This is especially important for students studying in a nonnative language (Daleure, 2012).

The Teaching-Learning Environment

As teachers in public tertiary institutions in the GCC, we prepare graduates to enter the technologically advanced workplaces of the region using English. Students must earn a specific International English Language Testing System overall Band 5 to meet the English language requirement for entry into bachelor degree programs. For most of our students, however, speaking achievement is often the highest and reading or writing are often lower by a full band or more (Wagie & Fox, 2005). Having their lowest proficiency in reading and writing corresponds with the overwhelming student preference for receiving oral communications and oral or visual instructions. These students also overwhelmingly prefer to express themselves orally or in visual digital formats rather than by writing. Students may understand spoken words but may not recognize the same words written on an instruction sheet or in a text or manual. Similarly, many of these students loathe writing.

Students in the GCC generally have underdeveloped reading and writing skills even in their native language, Arabic. In recent years, more emphasis has been given to developing reading skills at the elementary level, but the current cohort of tertiary education students has been more influenced by an oral literary tradition with a huge discrepancy between the spoken vernacular language and the formal written language (Raddawi, 2012).

Rapid integration of technology, including increased social media and mobile application technology usage, has contributed to the emergence of a hybrid language, Arabizi—phonetically representing Arabic words using English letters, often in a regional dialect. The informal written expression varies widely from individual to individual using hybrid English-Arabic grammatical structures. For example, we often receive emails with the words justified right instead of left (as Arabic is written from right to left), with words spelled phonetically in English. We have learned to "read using the students' voices" to glean the meaning from email messages.

When faced with formal writing assignments with the expectation of accuracy in spelling and grammar, many of our students complain and ultimately achieve less than desirable outcomes. Experiences of teachers in the GCC are exemplified by Alabad and Gitsaki (2011) and Daleure (2011), who suggested that the new technology-assisted writing style, combined with the oral learning tradition, leads students to perceive formal or academic reading as boring or cumbersome, whether it be in formal written Arabic or in English.

Flipping Our Classrooms

In past semesters, the English for Specific Purposes course was dreaded by many students, some of whom barely passed their prerequisite course, Academic Reading and Writing I. The main aim of the English for Specific Purposes course is to prepare engineering technology students to produce written technical reports as a part of their capstone projects. With only 4 contact hours per week, most of the instructional time involved showing students how to write technical reports, with students working on a sample report on their own outside class, the major problem being that the students at this stage of their college career were not working on engineering projects that required reports of this level. As such, we needed to find a way to make the whole process more "real" for them.

Experiential Projects

During a professional development workshop, we learned about the potential of using the flipped classroom. We decided to restructure the course to free up about 50% of the class time to use in experiential activities. To do this, we studied the syllabus and identified areas that could be prerecorded. We chose Camtasia to record lessons on how to create the report template, chose Quizlet activities for vocabulary input, and selected automated PowerPoint slide presentations for grammar input.

In the following section, we discuss one project, building a Rube-Goldberg machine (Kim & Park, 2012) to demonstrate the law of Conservation of Energy. The project was divided into several stages, each containing integration of vocabulary, content, and reinforcement of concepts previously taught in the Academic Reading and Writing I course. It is important to note that the English teachers did not teach the physics concepts. Our task, as language teachers, was to guide students through the process of effectively expressing their experiences in oral and written English.

Experiential Project Example: The Rube-Goldberg Machine

To begin, we explained to the students that they would have to complete this project and produce a report, and we emphasized that the format of the report would be similar to that of the capstone project report. This established a clear and pressing need for students to engage in the course. We also instructed them to keep a video log of each stage (planning, building, analysis, and rebuilding) to help them when writing the report.

In their first flipped lesson, the students received a model report layout in PDF format through Blackboard Learn. Then, via video, we guided students through the basic format (Cover Page, Headings, Table of Contents, and References Page). In the following class, we checked their templates, revisited areas where most had made errors, and encouraged those students who were more technologically advanced to help their peers to resolve various remaining formatting problems. We then used the report layout to introduce students to the content of the various sections. Following this, we introduced The Law of Conservation of Energy and explained that this would be included in the Background Theory for the first section.

In the next flipped lesson, we provided students with links to videos on energy transfer versus energy transformation and how energy is never created or lost. After that, in class, we gave students questions on the topic to elicit discussion. This was followed by group work, with each group tasked with collating the information learned, organizing it, and writing it up in the Background Theory section of the report. We advised students to use the correct citations and construct a references list. Again, the more confident students were allowed to assist their classmates, reinforcing the group dynamic.

The project work continued in this way over a 6-week period, with the flipped lessons being used to provide input for ideas on elements students could then include when building their machine, and recorded PowerPoint slide shows covering grammar elements they would need to help them describe how the machine worked.

Students produced work throughout the stages of the machine construction. The experiential nature of the lessons enabled students to interact with us so that we could check that they knew and were using the necessary language for the project. For example, as a part of their machine was completed, we could ask how they had built it, what problems they had had, how they had solved these, and how that particular part worked. In that way, student work served as formative assessment tools for us while also providing a valuable reference for the students' future projects.

Reflections on the Experience

We observed that the lessons encouraged active learning through increased student interest in the subject and motivation to build their own machine. Teachers commented that they really valued the time to get to know the students and see them in a new light. Working with the students while they built their machines and constructed their reports allowed for an opportunity to view students really interested in their work.

Constructing the video log was perhaps the most valuable part of the course because students could review it as many times as needed to construct their report. One teacher remarked, "I did not have a single paper that I doubted was written by the student." Another teacher remarked,

❝ I have seen the confidence level skyrocket mostly because it was genuine, students were genuinely interested in expressing themselves and felt that they could. ❞

Feedback from students indicated that they initially felt that the experience was time-consuming and unfamiliar to them. They were not used to accessing self-study materials, but, after a few lessons, they realized that they needed the input prior to the lesson to complete the class-based activity that they perceived as relevant and fun. As the tasks unfolded, the students realized that the just-in-time language input enabled them to better articulate their experience orally and in written form. At the mid-term, students were given an opportunity to give feedback on the course and specifically the "new" way of learning. One student remarked, "I think Arab students prefer doing speaking to reading." Another student in the group pointed out, "We did the individual first and then the group work but I think it is better to do the group first and then the individual so we can all learn from each other, then do it alone." We noted this advice for the next running of the course.

The process of recording the videos enabled students to develop healthy practices of reviewing and revisiting their work using a model. One student remarked,

> ❝ When we do something, and then we write, it helps to make our writing better. It helps to focus. ❞

Having a rich pool of self-access study materials enabled students with gaps in their learning to effectively keep up with the class. Overall, student input was positive and the writing of students improved significantly from the prerequisite Academic Reading and Writing I course to the English for Specific Purposes course.

Conclusion

Adult learning theory states that to enhance adult learning, a direct link must be made between the learning outcome and a practical application of the learning outcome. English as a second language theory emphasizes the importance of contextually relevant interaction between teachers and learners and among learners. In this project, we tried to incorporate the best of adult learning theory with the best of English as a second language theory. During the course implementation process, we realized that we had to continually refine our approaches to the videos and the classwork. We had to assure that videos were pitched at the correct level and were of a consistently high quality. We also learned that in class, we had to check on whether students had watched the videos in their entirety and took notes. In some cases, we added self-assessment tasks and coursework weighting because our students sometimes perceived activities without marks as unimportant.

It took a while for the students to accept the approach, mostly because it was new, but also because they were more used to being tested on what they had already done. At the end of the course, however, the students and teachers expressed that they felt that the experiential learning experience and flipped classroom approach added value to their learning experience. In the words of a graduating student, "When we came to the final project we remembered how to reference graphs, charts and pictures, you know Fig 1 etc." Another student added, "I kept the template, so it helped with the layout for the final report," and a third student admitted,

> ❝ We enjoyed the practical. It made it more fun and a challenge, but at first it was a challenge because it was different from other lessons. ❞

Another student in the same group explained,

> In other courses, out of class lessons were mostly quizzes and tests, [in this class] we had to get used to getting information from the videos ourselves and understanding what it meant. We had to be more active, not just watching, sometimes we had to take notes or make a picture, but once we got it, we got it!

....

Andrew Downer is academic coordinator at Sharjah Men's College, Higher Colleges of Technology, Sharjah, United Arab Emirates.

Dr. Georgia Daleure is program chair of General Studies at Sharjah Colleges, Higher Colleges of Technology, Sharjah, United Arab Emirates.

References

Alabad, A., & Gitsaki, C. (2011). Attitudes toward learning English: A case study of university students in Saudi Arabia. In C. Gitsaki (Ed.), *Teaching and learning in the Arab world* (pp. 3–28). Bern, Switzerland: Peter Lang.

Bishop, L., & Verleger, M. (2013, June). *The flipped classroom: A survey of the research.* Paper presented at the 120th ASEE Annual Conference & Exposition. Atlanta, GA: American Society for Engineering Education

Dale, E. (1969). *Audiovisual methods in teaching.* New York, NY: Dryden Press.

Daleure, G. (2011, November). Maximizing the effectiveness of classroom teaching with second language business students: The power punch of blended learning. In S. P. Horn, B. Stetar, M. Gordon, M. Esposito, J. Kahlman, H. Reed, & D. Saral (Eds.), *International Council for Business Schools and Programs (ACBSP) annual conference proceedings: Sustaining excellence through quality business education* (Vol. 1, Iss. 3; pp. 376–386). Overland Park, KS: Association of Collegiate Business Schools and Programs.

Daleure, G. (2012). Blended learning for success in the UAE knowledge-based economy. *E-Learning in Action, 1,* 1–10.

Kim, Y., & Park, N. (2012). Elementary education of creativity improvement using Rube Golberg's invention. In Y. Kim & N. Park (Eds.), Information technology convergence: Secure and trust computing, and data management (pp. 257–263). Singapore: Springer.

Raddawi, R. (2011). Teaching critical thinking to Arab University students. In C. Gitsaki (Ed.), *Teaching and learning in the Arab world* (pp. 71–92). Bern, Switzerland: Peter Lang.

Wagie, D., & Fox, W. (2005). Transforming education in the UAE: Contributing to social progress and the new economy. International Journal of Learning, 12(7), 268–277.

CHAPTER

11 Peer Mentoring Among ESL Learners via a Social Networking Site

RADZUWAN AB. RASHID

A dvances in information and communication technology allow the emergence of innovative pedagogical practices in supporting student learning. One example of these practices is online peer mentoring, which encourages peer-to-peer interaction to exchange information, acquire new knowledge, and support the learning process. Feiman-Nemser (2012) refers to this form of mentoring as an "informal buddy system" in which the mentor usually gives advice for technical issues and shows support for emotional issues.

I chose Facebook as the social networking site (SNS) for my mentoring project because it is widely used in Malaysia, where I teach. As of July 2013, there were 13.3 million Facebook users, making it the most popular SNS in the country (Mahadi, 2013). Most of these users are students in secondary schools, colleges, and universities. Besides using Facebook for learning purposes, Malaysian youth also use Facebook for online shopping (Suki, Ramayah, & Ly, 2012), constructing desired self-images (Rashid, 2016), and creating and sustaining friendship (Rashid & Rahman, 2014). I hypothesized that Facebook would be a convenient platform for engagement in the mentoring process, because the site has long been integrated in students' daily lives.

Contextualizing the Project

I had two purposes for this peer-mentoring project: (1) to provide an alternative medium to students who feel shy to engage in face-to-face discussion and (2) to give autonomy to students to organize their own learning. The project involved 20 Diploma TESL (teaching English as a second language) students taking the course Introduction to Pre-School Education at the Universiti Sultan Zainal Abidin (UniSZA), Malaysia. Altogether, there were 99 TESL students taking this course, and there was a wide gap in the students' academic achievement. Some of them scored very high cumulative grade point averages of 3.7 and above (high achievers), and some of them scored as low as 2.7 (low achievers).

I chose the 20 participants (10 low achievers, 10 high achievers) for this project using purposive sampling. The high achievers were assigned the roles of mentor and the low achievers were assigned the roles of mentee. The high achievers shared the following common characteristics: They actively took part in classroom activities, and they were friendly and approachable. The selected low achievers were passive participants in classroom activities and often shy to express themselves in English. I chose online mentoring instead of face-to-face mentoring because the majority of students were in various geographic locations.

At the very beginning of the mentoring process, I introduced each mentor and mentee pair face-to-face. In this introductory session, I briefed them about the concept of peer mentoring and raised their awareness of the importance of collaboration in the learning process. I also informed them that they needed to work together outside of academic hours for 8 weeks, using Facebook as the platform of interaction.

Recent Approaches to Mentoring

The word *mentor* originally refers to "a *father figure* who sponsors, guides and develops a younger person" (Ehrich, Hansford, & Tennent, 2004, p. 521). In the context of teaching within higher education, peer mentoring can be generally defined as a collaborative process of developing students' knowledge and skills in which the students are paired with more advanced learners (Ruane & Koku, 2014). Through peer mentoring, students have the opportunity to work closely with the more knowledgeable colleague to support their learning.

Peer mentoring is rather a new concept compared to "classic mentoring" (Liu, Macintyre, & Ferguson, 2012), in which mentors must be someone who is older and more knowledgeable than the mentees. Smith (2007) highlights two important characteristics of peer mentoring: (1) It can involve individuals who are equal in status and in age, such as a coworker or a peer; and (2) in terms of knowledge, the mentor can be more experienced than the mentee or at the same developmental level. This is based on the assumption that learning occurs collegially and socially through discourse with others and is mediated by the differences in coparticipants' perspectives (Wenger, 2010).

A successful mentoring process develops trust, friendship, and a safe environment for learners to negotiate meaning (Munby & Russell, 1989; Rashid, 2014). However, not all learners have equal access to mentoring (Bierema & Merriam, 2002) because of various hurdles, especially time and distance constraints (Long, 1997). Feiman-Nemser (2012) points out that a common challenge among many teachers is that they have insufficient time to spend on mentoring because of noninstructional duties and "needy students" (p. 14). Student teachers face similar problems in which they are occupied with tasks and coursework while at the same time they need to take part in curricular activities required by the university.

Bierema and Merriam (2002) argue that the problems affecting equal access to mentoring can be controlled through e-mentoring, such as using e-mail and chat groups. They define e-mentoring as "a computer mediated, mutually beneficial relationship between a mentor and a protégé which provides learning, advising, encouraging, promoting, and modeling, that is often boundaryless, egalitarian, and qualitatively different than traditional face-to-face mentoring" (p. 214). This definition challenges the conventional conceptualization that mentoring must be based on personal, face-to-face meetings. In addition, this definition also suggests that mentoring should cross the barriers of hierarchy, race, gender, age, and geography that are hardly crossed in traditional mentoring processes (Bierema & Merriam, 2002). The shift in mentoring from face-to-face to online contexts requires the mentor and mentee to "unlearn embedded notions of mentoring and conceptualize mentoring in new ways" (Gardner, 2009, p. 56). In other words, the mentors and mentees must learn that they do not have to wait for the opportunity to see each other in person for them to work together. With this in mind, I set out to raise my students' awareness to make full use of SNSs and introduced the notion of online peer mentoring to them.

Ensher, Heun, and Blanchard (2003) provide a useful typology of online mentoring that helps to distinguish different kinds of participation in the mentoring process. They describe the first type as "computer-mediated-communication [CMC]-only," or "CMC-only," referring to a mentoring process that is only online, such as by using email, websites, chat rooms, and instant messaging. In the second type, "CMC-primary," the majority of mentoring interactions are conducted online, but the mentors and mentees may sometimes engage in telephone calls and face-to-face interactions. In the final type, "CMC-supplemental," the majority of mentoring is done face-to-face and the relationship is supplemented via online interactions. In this project, I experimented with CMC-only mentoring, as my initial observations revealed that the students were often on Facebook. This made me feel that the students would be happy to talk to one another through the site.

Student Feedback on Peer Mentoring Through a Social Networking Site

Advantages

As the group interviews revealed, using Facebook for peer mentoring has several advantages. The first and main advantage is the flexible learning outside the classroom; students highlighted that they can interact with each other at their own convenience.

> I woke up at 2am and cannot sleep. I scroll down the Facebook message, responding to my mentor's question and asking her some new questions. This is so convenient. No need to travel, no need to change my clothes. I have my own personal space but able to engage in interpersonal activity. (Murni)[1]

Previous studies on peer mentoring using online platforms support the finding that participants value the opportunity to take part in learning any time and anywhere (e.g., Rashid & Rahman, 2014; Ensher et al., 2003). Additionally, though institutional platforms may provide a more structured/organized learning experience than Facebook, students reported that they have a higher tendency to log on to Facebook compared with the institutional platform, primarily because the site's interface is customized for various types of gadgets, such as smartphone and tablet. In contrast, an institutional platform (e.g., KeLiP) produces a less appealing interface when opened using a smartphone. These findings indicate that an informal SNS, such as Facebook, can be as effective as other institutional online platforms in providing a flexible learning experience to the students.

However, some students pointed out that given an option, they would prefer to use WhatsApp Messenger over Facebook because they feel that it has friendlier user interface design. In addition, they reported that other features on Facebook, such as status updates, comments, and photos, can sometimes be distracting. To some extent, this finding contradicts Wade, Niederhauser, Cannon, and Long (2001), who argue that online platforms promote more task-oriented interaction than face-to-face contexts.

The second advantage of using Facebook is the archive, which enables users to refer to the earlier discussion. As pointed out by Ensher et al. (2003), having written discussion is beneficial because the students can revisit what they have discussed. The students highly value the record of interaction:

---

[1] Student names are pseudonyms.

We found that having the interactions recorded on the website is very useful. In face-to-face mentoring, you might forget what your mentor says or you might need to be busy jotting down till you cannot focus. Having the interactions written on the site is useful because you can refer back to them. It is also helpful to keep track of our progress. (Syura)

The third advantage is the delayed (rich) response afforded by the asynchronous chat function. The students highlighted that were able to provide meaningful responses to their partner's inquiries because they have more time to think and search for supporting evidence online. Tiqa, who was shy when participating in lessons and was assigned the role of a mentee, gave the following response:

> ❝ I usually don't have confidence to respond because I often feel I have very limited knowledge on particular issues. Since the mentoring is done on Facebook, I can read the questions first and then take my own time to search for info on Google to support my response. So when I click enter, I click with confidence because I know there is substance in my response. ❞ (Tiqa)

The benefit of delayed responses highlighted by the participants in this study resonates with Wade et al. (2001), who argue that online mentoring is more effective than face-to-face mentoring because it facilitates more thoughtful responses. Wade et al. (2001) are critical of responses in face-to-face mentoring, which can be too spontaneous to address complex problems.

Another interesting advantage put forth by the students is that the peer mentoring through Facebook enables them to improve upon an existing and perhaps lackluster friendship. This is in contrast to Ensher et al. (2003), who point out that online mentoring can cause a problematic relationship, especially because of emotionally charged writing, or what they refer to as "flaming." Successful mentoring leads to the development of trust and friendship (Munby & Russell, 1989). Liza was paired with a mentee whom she perceived as problematic, but they gradually developed a good relationship, as evident in the following excerpt.

> When you asked me to work with her on Facebook, I feel like WHAT??? Hahaha. But because this is an academic activity, I know I need to be professional. So I give it a go. It is quite awkward at the beginning to discuss with someone that you have problems with.

> ❝ I cannot imagine if this is a face-to-face mentoring. I might not have the courage to take part in this mentoring activity. As time goes by, I think we started to feel more comfortable to talk to each other. It is good to befriend her again, both on Facebook and in the real life. ❞ (Liza)

Disadvantages

Online peer mentoring through Facebook has distinctive disadvantages. The main disadvantage is related to the depth of discussion; students reported that Facebook is not an appropriate platform for detailed academic interaction and it is less engaging than face-to-face discussion, which can result in lower levels of student involvement.

> ❝ I don't think I like discussing academic matter through Facebook. It is a very dry space. We want to interact, speak, not just typing out. It is not fun. No gesture, no eye contact. As for face-to-face mentoring, you can see reactions. ❞

> But on Facebook if someone types very long, which rarely happens, I won't bother to read. Then I just say I agree. So kind of low level of involvement from us. We don't even feel that we need to perform our best when discussing on SNS. (Yana)

As suggested by Ensher et al. (2003), written online mentoring can be less engaging because it does not allow students to see body language, hear tone of voice, or infer meaning from a variety on nonverbal cues. This suggests that the various emoticons created by Facebook are not sufficient in producing the effects of personal human contact afforded by face-to-face interaction.

Another problem with using Facebook for mentoring is the higher probability of miscommunication. Often, participants assumed that they understood the responses given and did not ask for clarification. It was only when they continued the discussion face-to-face that they realized they did not correctly understand some responses.

> My mentor asked me to email her the resources that I referred to. So I sent three articles to her. The three that I thought are the most influential. But when we met in the class, she said I was asking for the complete list of references, not the full articles. (Kamal)

King and Engi (1998) point out the possibility of misunderstanding attempts at humor, misreading tone, or failing to clarify understanding. Seeing this finding verified in my context was surprising, as I tried to counter this occurrence by pairing students with classmates they have known for four semesters. That such miscommunications still occurred implies that misinterpretation is likely when the students interact through written communication regardless of how long they have known each other.

All the participants in this study agreed that SNSs such as Facebook should only be used to supplement face-to-face interaction in the mentoring process. For instance, Fazry said, "To get information through SNS is okay, but to understand more and to get explanation, I prefer face-to-face. To understand something through a long text is very difficult because of ambiguity etcetera. I don't want to discuss via Facebook all the time."

It is clear to me now my students prefer Ensher et al.'s (2003) CMC-supplemental type of mentoring. Rather than interacting online only or even mostly online, they prefer a type of mentoring in which the majority of interactions are face-to-face and the mentoring is supplemented via online platforms.

Conclusion

Engaging students in peer mentoring using informal networking sites, such as Facebook, has its own advantages and disadvantages. Similar to formal online platforms, Facebook promotes a flexible learning experience where the students can take part in the learning process at their own convenience. Because Facebook enables students to have their own personal space, it also helps students who feel shy participating in face-to-face interaction to take part in the mentoring process. Contrary to findings in several previous studies, which show that online mentoring can be detrimental to mentor-mentee relationships, I found that Facebook is useful in developing the relationship. However, engaging students in thorough discussions on the site can be challenging, as they tend to give short responses, which add to the risk of misinterpretation and miscommunication.

After listening to the voices of my students, I have to conclude—much to my surprise—that Facebook should only be used to supplement face-to-face interactions for mentoring to be effective. I thought that because most of my students spend so much time on Facebook, they would be happy to informally discuss their academic matters on the site. However, this was not the case. What I learned from this project is that SNSs cannot simply be incorporated in the classroom by teachers in a top-down fashion. Rather, such integration requires a careful negotiation with students. In short, students need a voice in how an SNS should be used to enhance their learning process.

....

Radzuwan Ab. Rashid is a senior lecturer in Faculty of Languages and Communication at Universiti Sultan Zainal Abidin, Kuala Terengganu, Malaysia.

References

Bierema, L. L., & Merriam, S. B. (2002). E-mentoring: Using computer mediated communication to enhance the mentoring process. *Innovative Higher Education, 26*(3), 211–227.

Ehrich, L. C., Hansford, B., & Tennent, L. (2004). Formal mentoring programs in education and other professions: A review of the literature. *Educational Administration Quarterly, 40*(4), 518–540.

Ensher, E. A., Heun, C., & Blanchard, A. (2003). Online mentoring and computer-mediated communication: New directions in research. *Journal of Vocational Behavior, 63*(2), 264–288.

Feiman-Nemser, S. (2012). Beyond solo teaching. *Educational Leadership, 69*(8), 10–16.

Gardner, H. (2009). *Five minds for the future.* Boston, MA: Harvard Business School Press.

King, S., & Engi, S. (1998). Using the Internet to assist family therapy. *British Journal of Guidance and Counselling, 26,* 43–53.

Liu, H., Macintyre, R. & Ferguson, R. (2012). Exploring qualitative analytics for e-mentoring relationships building in an online social learning environment. In S. Buckingham Shum, D. Gasevic, & R. Ferguson (Eds.), *Proceedings of the 2nd International Conference on Learning Analytics and Knowledge* (pp. 179–183). New York, NY: Association for Computing Machinery.

Long, J. (1997). The dark side of mentoring. *Australian Educational Research, 24,* 115–123.

Mahadi, N. (2013, June 16). 13.3 million M'sians are Facebook users. *Borneo Post.* Retrieved from http://www.theborneopost.com/2013/06/16/13-3-million-msians-are-facebook-users/

Munby, H., & Russell, T. (1989). *Teachers and teaching: From classroom to reflection.* London, England: Falmer Press.

Rashid, R. A. (2014). *Exploring methodological and ethical issues in researching teachers' informal learning on a social networking site.* Nottingham, England: The Nottingham Jubilee Press.

Rashid, R. A. (2016). Topic continuation strategies employed by teachers in managing supportive conversations on Facebook timeline. *Discourse Studies, 18*(2), 1–18.

Rashid, R. A., & Rahman, M. F. (2014). Social networking sites for online mentoring and creativity enhancement. *International Journal of Technology Enhanced Learning, 6*(1), 34–45.

Ruane, R., & Koku, E. F. (2014). Social network analysis of undergraduate education student interaction in online peer mentoring settings. *MERLOT Journal of Online Learning and Teaching, 10*(4), 577–589.

Smith, A. (2007). Mentoring for experienced school principals: Professional learning in a safe place. *Mentoring and Tutoring, 15*(3), 277–291.

Suki, N. M., Ramayah, T., & Ly, K. K. (2012). Empirical investigation on factors influencing the behavioral intention to use Facebook. *Universal Access in the Information Society, 11*(2), 223–231.

Wade, S., Niederhauser, D. S., Cannon, M., & Long, T. (2001). Electronic discussions in an issue course: Expanding the boundaries of the classroom. *Journal of Computing in Teacher Education, 17*(3), 4–9.

Wenger, E. (2010). Communities of practice and social learning systems: the career of a concept. In C. Blackmore (Ed.), *Social learning systems and communities of practice* (pp.179–198). London, England: Springer.

12 Future Directions for Online and Hybrid Language Learning

GREG KESSLER

From Established to New Forms

This collection illustrates a diversity of TESOL educational contexts that benefit from online and hybrid delivery. Obviously, there are many opportunities related to these new instructional formats for both students and teachers. Besides allowing participants to collaborate and engage with course content from anywhere at any time, the varied interpretations of online and hybrid learning included in this book demonstrate the extensive opportunities available to teachers and students to reflect on their practice. The participant voices recorded here are from diverse contexts as well as a broad geographical and pedagogical range. Until recently, these types of online and hybrid experiences have relied upon established tools and environments that might be considered first-generation online learning contexts. The particular significance of this volume is that many of the chapters extend beyond the previous boundaries. This tells me that online and hybrid language learning will be taking on many new forms in the near future.

A number of chapters present diverse approaches to online and hybrid collaboration and point to the emergence of technological developments that may significantly influence the classrooms of the future. Many of these developments are technologies that create wholly new social and communicative experiences. Others rely on the expansion of big data and development of tools that allow us to utilize these datasets in meaningful ways. We can anticipate that participants will want to take advantage of many of these new opportunities, and we should anticipate that future investigations into practice will resemble the studies in this volume in their creative attempts to address a range of educational challenges. As technologies evolve and new functionalities emerge, teachers will always recognize new ways to adapt and integrate these tools. This chapter presents an overview of a variety of emerging and potential technologies and functionalities that are on the horizon for English as a second language (ESL), English as a foreign language (EFL), and TESOL teacher preparation classrooms of the future.

Emerging Issues

Technological Transparency

Chapters in this volume describe varied contexts, and as English language teaching and learning technologies and practices evolve, more diversity will result. Our experience and expectations of online tools and related social practices are still in a nascent stage. Though teachers and students are very conscious of technology in current online learning and are often faced with technology-specific challenges, they should expect a more transparent experience in the future (Bax, 2011). This simply means that technology is becoming less obvious as we become more accustomed to using it. Ideally, teachers will become so comfortable with technology when teaching that it will be no more noticeable than using a print book or blackboard.

Learning and Content Management

There are also some ongoing and emerging trends that are not thoroughly captured by chapters in this volume. Authors throughout this collection describe dramatic developments regarding online learning tools and their use. Learning management systems (LMSs) are now used to organize course materials in a manner that is easy to navigate. This includes opportunities to track, report, and assess students and courses. Most learning and content management systems share many characteristics and functions, such as registration, scheduling, content delivery and tracking, communication, recording grades, tests, and assignments.

Blackboard, Moodle, and Sakai are among the most popular LMSs. These systems are becoming increasingly interactive, allowing a participatory, active, and interactive environment for students and teachers. Students particularly appreciate the LMS environment's role in developing their learning, communication, and collaboration (Carvalho, Areal, & Silva, 2011). Consequently, it is important for teachers who develop courses within an LMS to focus on utilizing communication and collaboration tools to meet their students' needs.

Further, the growth in online and hybrid learning has resulted in a need to develop meaningful approaches to assessing the quality of such instruction. However, measuring quality is a complicated and sometimes unclear task. Experts in online learning and assessment do not always agree on definitions of quality or how to measure it. Quality may be perceived differently for students, instructors, administrators, or accrediting bodies. Some think that online course quality can be determined in the same manner as face-to-face classes, but others argue that online teaching represents more than just an alternate delivery mode. Rather, they think it should be considered as a wholly new instructional approach, including new teaching, learning, and assessment methods. To further complicate things, some have suggested that teachers need to reflect upon cultural and cultural-pedagogical constructs when developing approaches to evaluating online learning quality.

Navigating such complex decisions can be challenging and even overwhelming. One valuable resource that can help in such circumstances is The TESOL Technology Standards (Healey et al., 2011). These standards provide benchmarks for teachers and learners in regard to technology use. A complete program evaluation is included to establish a better understanding of instructors' technology abilities in order to determine appropriate goals for future development. Vignettes are also included to illustrate technology integration across various contexts, language levels, and variations of technology access. These can easily be adopted or adapted for online and hybrid teaching contexts. The standards also provide guidelines for evaluating the effectiveness of online and hybrid teaching.

Telecollaboration

One area that deserves more attention is telecollaboration. Essentially, all telecollaborative exchanges involve using technology as a common environment for two groups to engage with one another around the experience of language learning. In this volume, Chapters 2 and 11 are both based upon telecollaboration frameworks. There are so many different ways to tellecollaborate that they are commonly referred to using different terms, including online intercultural exchanges, cross-cultural exchanges, keypal projects, and, most recently, virtual exchanges. Telecollaboration can take the form of one-to-one exchanges between individual pairs of students or class-to-class exchanges that allow entire classes to interact. They can be monolingual or multilingual. They can focus specifically on language learning or incorporate language learning within the context of learning about some other topic that is socially, culturally, or academically relevant to the pursuits of the students involved. Various forms of telecollaboration have created a number of new opportunities for language instructors over the past two decades.

Though there is much variety, these exchanges tend to share a focus on utilizing the various computer-mediated communication modes that are familiar today, such as synchronous and asynchronous text, audio, and video exchange. Synchronous communication takes place in real time and includes tweeting, texting, videoconferencing, and even telephone conversations. These activities require participants to process language quickly and respond without too much hesitation. Asynchronous communication, such as email, blogs, wikis, and audio and video archiving, allow students to spend more time reflecting on what has been said in order to respond more thoroughly and thoughtfully. Both modes of communication are important for students to learn.

Studies about telecollaboration have observed that students demonstrate increased motivation and overall linguistic output. It has been noted that students in telecollaborative exchanges have greater access to authentic forms of communication using authentic tools and language. Such authentic experiences have been found to contribute to student motivation and engagement and help to make class activities feel relevant. These exchanges have been recognized for promoting a student-centered learning environment. They have also observed improvements in fluency, accuracy, autonomy, pragmatics, and perhaps most commonly intercultural communicative competence.

One of the most common goals in telecollaborative projects has been the learning of culture. In fact, many telecollaboration projects are designed specifically to improve students' intercultural communicative competence, and this platform can provide unique access to other cultural domains in a variety of ways. Most recently, a number of these kinds of exchanges are intentionally focused on preparing students to engage in socially responsible ways within the domains of gaming and social media. Such projects help students develop various online literacies while also practicing their language skills. Introducing gaming and game-related concepts into education has become quite popular across disciplines in recent years. Some have observed the informal collaborative creation of online groups of gamers for the specific purpose of language learning. This has inspired some instructors to attempt to mimic or adopt these gaming practices within formal language education. We may see online and hybrid courses in the future that take place completely within gaming contexts.

There has also been a recent increase in the number of telecollaboration projects that are centered around language teacher preparation. These kinds of exchanges can offer preservice teachers opportunities to experiment with and explore these increasingly varied instructional domains to evaluate their instructional potential. Teachers can also benefit from improving their abilities with multimodal technologies as they engage in these exchanges, and they are able to access experts in the field who are not available locally.

However, there have been a number of challenges associated with telecollaboration. Perhaps the greatest of these is the simple fact that these exchanges tend to take place in an ad hoc manner that is peripheral to programmatic, departmental, or institutional goals, thus limiting the importance and potential impact of such projects. The logistics of coordinating these exchanges has also been noted as exceptionally challenging. To rely upon such an exchange, instructors need to have an established relationship with representatives from partnering institutions. In some cases, it may be necessary to know a number of people at the partner institution in case of absence, competing commitments, or cultural conflicts. Even under these circumstances, problems are likely to arise that require creative solutions. Many of the numerous papers and books about this topic focus on these varied challenges.

Massive Open Online Courses

The developments in online learning tools, along with experience in telecollaboration, have contributed to the explosion of massive open online courses (MOOCs). Perhaps the most noticeable recent trend in online learning, MOOCs are designed to accommodate large numbers of participants, typically for free and with open-ended outcomes. MOOCs integrate accessible online resources, social networking, and a number of automated functions that allow the simultaneous accommodation of many participants. They are often also facilitated by uniquely talented and recognized experts in a discipline. In some specific contexts, particularly engineering and computer science, MOOCs have been a substantial disruptive force in education. Many have anticipated similar disruptions in other domains as well, including English language teaching.

Thus far, English language teaching through MOOCs is somewhat underrepresented, but there have been significant developments in this area. A quick search on MOOC List (www.mooc-list.com) reveals hundreds of current MOOCs for English language learning and teaching. Many of these may provide readers with access to a new community of thought about the profession.

The U.S. Department of State has sponsored the creation of English language teaching and learning MOOCs the past few years. They recognize the potential for this context to reach young people around the world who are interested in both learning and teaching English. The potential to reach so many individuals through one course is exhilarating and promising, but there are numerous challenges associated with MOOCs. Many have expressed their concern about the attrition rate, which is often as high as 90–95% of students initially enrolled! Some have suggested that this is largely due to the generic and sterile nature of an environment that is designed to be a one-size-fits-all solution. Many who are involved in the world of MOOCs are seeking solutions, such as introducing more varied materials, including various cultural informants, and integrating a variety of technologies that are designed to improve the learner experience.

Automated Feedback

Some of the technologies that have been developed to support MOOCs have already found their way into more conventional online and hybrid courses. One example of this includes tools that have been developed for automated writing evaluation (AWE). Because of the large class size in a MOOC, there is a need for student-produced texts to be assessed and responded to in an automated manner using natural language processing tools. While there is some controversy around these approaches because of the complex nature of human writing, these tools have become sophisticated enough to provide reliable feedback for limited contexts and purposes.

AWE has witnessed many advances in recent years. Research into AWE has revealed that students find it helpful and motivating, but not as useful as peer feedback or feedback from an instructor. Ware (2011) found AWE tools to be reliable within specific genres and contexts, particularly those that align with formulaic writing, such as a five-paragraph essay. There are also a number of challenges associated with AWE, including too much of a focus on local errors at the expense of global issues as well as a tendency to defer to formulaic writing conventions. There is consensus among those who have developed and observed AWE tools that informed teachers can greatly enhance their implementation. In fact, it seems that when these systems do not function effectively, it is not the fault of the technology, but inadequate or inappropriate teacher training and support (Li, Link, & Hegelheimer, 2015). Consequently, it is important for language teachers to understand AWE so they can make effective decisions about implementation.

Automated systems that are designed specifically for language instruction rely on natural language processing and learner modeling, which utilize static properties about learners as a means of predicting future performance, such as first language, learning style preferences, and previous learner performance. Such information allows designers to achieve an ideal prioritization of feedback within the system. These systems are increasingly capable of presenting students with interactive experiences that provide salient feedback at important moments in the learning process.

Though these tools do offer us new opportunities to deliver individualized and customized feedback at specific points in instruction, it still seems that students respond more positively to feedback from an instructor and utilize such feedback more as they revise their writing. Further, instructors often have insights into individual learner characteristics, including sociolinguistic, strategic, and discourse competencies that may temper how they present feedback. As a result, we should anticipate that instructors will continue to play an important and changing role in these learning contexts. This realization emphasizes the importance for instructors to develop new abilities and skills to adapt these emerging tools to their teaching contexts.

Importantly, we must identify which of these aspects can be reliably automated and what an instructor needs to do to integrate them effectively (Kessler, 2013). It is not obvious how teachers need to integrate the emerging array of automated tools that can be used for language evaluation and feedback, but we will certainly be encountering more of these kind of tools in the near future. Those who are involved in researching such projects anticipate significant developments in the near future in terms of reliability as well as an improved awareness of the role of teachers in mediating and interpreting automated feedback (Ware, 2014). Such automated forms of evaluation are becoming increasingly common in standardized testing contexts, as well. When used in conjunction with qualified teachers who understand the abilities and limitations of such automated assessment, the potential for these tools is greatly enhanced. We should anticipate seeing more of these automated tools in online and hybrid classrooms as well as face-to-face contexts.

We should also expect that our experience and familiarity with these technologies and practices will mature and allow us to benefit more from the overall experience. The emergence of these new spaces and our increasing ability to use them effectively will contribute to a greater sense of engagement in these learning experiences (Kessler, 2013). We should also expect that these new technologies will continue to require us to provide teachers with adequate and appropriate preparation to use them effectively. In fact, we may find such preparation more necessary in a future filled with numerous intelligent and sophisticated technologies.

Virtual Reality

Another example of an emerging context that requires attention is virtual reality. Future online and hybrid teachers will be able to virtually transport themselves and their students in a variety of socially meaningful ways. These practices will benefit from the previous work that has been done in the areas of simulation and gaming, which have constructed very similar experiences, albeit without the new convincing immersive sensory experience. Developments in virtual reality have made it possible for teachers and learners to experiment with creating landscapes that feel real and support extensive language practice (Reshad, Hendrickx, Schwartz, & Kessler, 2017).

In earlier simulation projects, Coleman (2002) described an extended lesson around the use of SIM COPTER in the context of teaching ESL writing at the university level. The simulation experience is constructed around two distinct perspectives of students in different roles. One student functions as a helicopter pilot while another functions as a visitor who is unfamiliar with the area. Because the visitor is unfamiliar with the surroundings, he or she is dependent upon the pilot, who has a bird's-eye view of the landscape. This scenario sets the stage for all kinds of exchanges demanding language use. In the study, students are directed to focus on the potential audience of their writing. Some of the other obvious tasks that are supported by this include giving and seeking directions to navigate the landscape, navigating around potentially threatening objects, or describing different aspects of the environment in detail. This scenario can also support a number of information-gap activities that extend beyond these basic tasks. As the Coleman (2002) notes, the role of audience is made more accessible and concretized through this experience.

With other emerging gaming, simulation, and virtual immersive contexts, we can anticipate myriad other ways that engaging activities can be constructed. We should also anticipate the emergence of wholly new environments and approaches that will present opportunities for immersive experiences that allow us to virtually engage in contexts relevant to target language and culture.

There is also an emergence of various mash-ups, or digital combinations, of virtual geographical tools with socially compelling data and a variety of opportunities to engage with others around this data. Yeh and Kessler (2015) explore a number of potential applications involving Google Earth, such as street view and other geolocation functionality, in conjunction with social media communication. They describe scenarios in which individuals are able to virtually visit a variety of remote locations, including historical sites, professional domains, and important cultural sites that can serve as a valuable contextual support for language learning practice. Students can navigate these remote environments while gathering location-specific information, interacting with the landscape, and engaging in problem-solving activities. The authors (Yeh & Kessler, 2015) focus on the ability of students to interact with others while sharing this virtual immersive geographical landscape, regardless of their physical location. We can certainly anticipate future online and hybrid learning benefiting from the incorporation of geographical context and associated information.

The varied potential for these new experiences is staggering, and TESOL professionals will need to stay abreast of these developments to provide their learners with optimal learning opportunities. We should definitely expect that future iterations of this volume will include many of these kind of projects. Similarly, we can anticipate a variety of developments in augmented reality, in which students and teachers who have a shared physical space can benefit from that environment being enhanced through the addition of augmented reality information. This information can be available in layers so that users can enable or disable it at their convenience. Layers may represent historical, geographical, social, or linguistic information. Users may engage in social activities that rely on this additional information as a prompt, or teachers can use augmented reality to distribute individualized information for various collaborative activities, such as jigsaw and information-gap activities. With this kind of enhancement, such activities could be constructed in a manner that allows them to serve as a major component of an entire class.

Artificial Intelligence

We should also anticipate that there will be significant influences in the areas of big data, artificial intelligence, and digital assistants that use this information to automate information gathering and menial tasks. The potential for artificial intelligence across education is almost too dramatic and vast to comprehend. With the expansion of big data, including the potential to treat the entire internet (or some selected subset of it) as a learning corpus provides teachers with authentic content and information that can be accessed or engaged with in many ways.

We now have digital assistants, such as Amazon's Echo and Google's Home, which are both designed to allow people to access information through oral and auditory interactions. In an early pilot study, I observed that teachers felt very comfortable introducing such devices into the classroom as a source of basic facts. This implementation can free teachers up to focus on other issues in the classroom while students gather information for various project-based activities. In distance learning contexts, such digital assistants could prove to be invaluable with such devices delivering individualized and customized instruction to students between online meetings with the instructor. We should anticipate more functionality across the artificial intelligence tools that can access this data. We should also anticipate the ability to construct meaningful customized subsets of data for specific activities, tasks, or individualized student needs.

Conclusion

Today we are just beginning to learn to navigate and utilize social media and the various forms of communication it supports. Consequently, many educators are reluctant or even afraid to implement social media because of concerns about security or ethics and because of a general discomfort with these new forms of media. We should anticipate that in the future we will all be much more familiar with these platforms and their implementation. As a result, we should expect their use to be safer for everyone involved.

We should anticipate that the use of these systems will become a standard procedure for TESOL instructors. We should also expect to have a greater ability to customize future social media domains for specific language learning projects. In addition, we will likely see more use of artificial intelligence within these contexts, providing students with automated feedback related to the authenticity of their content and the accuracy of their language production. Such developments will help us create new online and hybrid learning experiences that will benefit instructors and learners in numerous ways.

It is likely that these future experiences will be quite different from what we recognize today. In fact, we can even imagine a future in which the distinction between hybrid and online contexts are indistinguishable. It may be difficult to envision today, but such possibilities are already on the horizon. We can only begin to anticipate the kinds of issues teachers and students will face as a result of technological changes. However, one thing is for certain: We will always benefit from the voices of those who reflect meaningfully on their experiences within these expansive learning contexts.

....

Greg Kessler is an associate professor of instructional technology and linguistics at Ohio University.

References

Bax, S. (2011). Normalisation revisited: The effective use of technology in language education. *International Journal of Computer Assisted Language Learning and Teaching*, 1(2), 1–15. doi:10.4018/ijcallt.2011040101

Carvalho, A., Areal, N., & Silva, J. (2011). Students' perceptions of Blackboard and Moodle in a Portuguese university. *British Journal of Educational Technology*, 42(5), 824–841.

Coleman, D. W. (2002). On foot in SIM CITY: Using SIM COPTER as the basis for an ESL writing assignment. *Simulation and Gaming*, 33(2), 217–230.

Healey, D., Hanson-Smith, E., Hubbard, P., Iannou-Georgiou, S., Kessler, G., & Ware, P. (2011). TESOL technology standards: Description, implementation, integration. Alexandria, VA: Teachers of English to Speakers of Other Languages.

Kessler, G. (2013). Teaching ESL/EFL in a world of social media, mash-ups and hyper-collaboration. *TESOL Journal*, 4, 307–322. doi:10.11139/cj.30.3.307–322

Li, J., Link, S, & Hegelheimer, V. (2015). Rethinking the role of automated writing evaluation in ESL writing instruction. *Journal of Second Language Writing, 27*, 1–18.

Reshad, A., Hendrickx, J., Schwartz, A., & Kessler, G. (2017). Reflections on the virtual boardroom: Business presentations in the Holodeck. In P. Hubbard & S. Ioannou-Georgiou (Eds.), *Teaching English reflectively with technology* (pp. 124–133). Canterbury, England: IATEFL.

Ware, P. (2011). Computer-generated feedback on student writing. *TESOL Quarterly, 45*, 769–774.

Ware, P. (2014). Feedback for adolescent writers in the English classroom: Exploring pen-and-paper, electronic, and automated options. *Writing & Pedagogy, 6*(2), 223–249.

Yeh, E., & Kessler, G. (2015). Enhancing linguistic and intercultural competencies through the use of social network sites and Google Earth. In J. Keengwe (Ed.), *Promoting global literacy skills through technology-infused teaching and learning* (pp. 1–22). Hershey, PA: IGI Global.